# WHERE
# ANGELS
## ~ TREAD ~

# WHERE ANGELS TREAD

## THE STORY OF VIÑA MONTES

*200201*

BY
JAMIE ROSS

WITH A FOREWORD BY HUGH JOHNSON

Viña Montes
Chile

# ACKNOWLEDGEMENTS

MY FIRST THANKS must go to Douglas Murray of Viña Montes. Many years ago, he drove me across the Atacama desert and showed me his part of Chile, thus beginning a long friendship. The idea of this book was his, but I should add that I have had complete authorial independence during its writing. Apart from putting me right on factual detail, Douglas and his fellow founding partners at Viña Montes—Aurelio Montes, Alfredo Vidaurre and Pedro Grand—let me get on with the job as I saw fit, without interference. I should like to thank them all for their support for the project. Writing a book in London about a wine producer in Chile has presented some challenges of distance. The gap between subject and author has been narrowed considerably by the close attention and support of everyone at Montes. In particular, I should like to thank Vanessa Moreno, Carlos Serrano, Victor Baeza, Sonia Montanares, Alejandra Ramirez and Andrés Turner for their help.

At home, I have been lucky to have had close at hand the skills of Richard Pierce, who designed the book and so ably brought it to life. The biggest debt of gratitude I owe is to my wife Caroline for (amongst much) reading the draft as it developed, making invaluable comments, and for putting up with me during the whole process.

I should also like to thank the following for their kind input during the research for the book and its preparation:

Marchese Piero Antinori
Ana María Barahona
Pierre Beuchet
Sally Bishop
Professor Edmundo
 Bordeu
Nicolás Catena

Amalia Cebreiro
María Emilia Campos
Johnny Chan
Oz Clarke
Samuel Claro
Greta Coghill
Michael Cooper

Michael Cox

Elizabeth Diaz

Hubrecht Duijker

John Duval

Marnix Engels

His Excellency Señor
  Mariano Fernández

Peter Gago

Jorge García

Rafael Guilisasti

Alex Guarachi

James Halliday

Professor Emeritus
  Alejandro Hernández

Yasuhisa Hirose

Kitty Johnson

Lucy Johnson

Cathy Kitch

Hi Sang Lee

Ciro Lilla

Michel Marentette

Sanjay Menon

Christian Moueix

Dmitry Pinski

Jürg Reinger

David Sandys-Renton

Christophe Salin

Michael Schachner

Steven Spurrier

Ralph Steadman

Tom E. Smith

Margaret Snook

Rob Temple

Karolin Thomas

Ch'ng Poh Tiong

Miguel A. Torres

Ignacio Williamson

Clet Wong

Martin Wright

To Caroline, Rosanna, Cecily and Thomas

# Contents

# Foreword

THE WINE WORLD used to move in slow motion. You could turn your back for a decade, it seemed, turn round again and see the same scene; the wines, and their producers, more mature, but the wine list, the vine rows and the cellars virtually unchanged.

Not any more. Today it is possible for a man aged barely forty to have witnessed, and to chronicle, the entire history of a wine house, from concept to planting to launch, then to worldwide distribution and finally to worldwide acclaim.

Not any wine house. If the Montes story reads like a dream it is because it started that way, and then progressively came true. Its progenitors, you feel, must deliberately avoid pinching themselves, for fear of waking up to a small business and walls not covered with trophies. This book then, should reassure them. It is the sober chronicle of their success: dream first, then methods, gambles, stumbles, acceptance and realization.

I first met Aurelio and Douglas in phase one; dreamtime. They were working together at Viña San Pedro, and showed me round, an excursion recorded in a photograph in the book I was helping to research, Jan Read's *Chilean Wines*. I had just made the discovery of Chile's vinous treasure. It was my second visit; the first, in the 1970s, had showed me only what potential there must be, and what a lovely country Chile was. Now I was beginning to see that Chile's grapes are as good as any on earth. Here is my tasting note on what must have been an early Aurelio Cabernet: 'Attractive nose, sweet and resinous. A fairly big robust wine with good tannic thrust. Very well made, enjoyable and a good interpretation of Chilean style'. Measured rapture, you might say.

Douglas was ebullient, engaged, intensely one-to-one: an instant friend. I suggested my nephew Jamie should take in Chilean wine as part of his broader education. He went, met the Montes pair, and found himself their first representative in London. He went on into publishing, but the British agency has been in the same hands ever since. Jamie was the natural choice to tell the story. Even he must have been astonished as the details came out. How do you start what amounts to a Grand Cru (no, several Grands Crus) from scratch? How do you persuade people to take your wines seriously? How do you repeat the process round the world? What happens when everybody falls in love with your baby? Can you turn a few thousand bottles into a few hundred thousand, then a few million, without losing the essence?

I refer you to what follows for the answers.

Hugh Johnson

*'Chilean wines would not have achieved their reputation and their position world-wide without the vision and contribution of a great wine personality like Aurelio Montes.'*

Marchese Piero Antinori
Marchesi Antinori, Italy

*'Aurelio Montes has ushered in a new era for Chilean wines. His unrelenting pursuit of quality has shown the world the quality potential of this great winemaking country.'*

Nicolás Catena
Bodega Catena Zapata, Argentina

*'To follow the progress of Montes has been to follow the progress of Chile as a modern wine nation. They are always at the fore of any move into new regions and they are always blazing the trail with new, ambitious flavours and styles. And for me, a traveller from distant Europe, they are the most charming hosts—generous with their time, generous with their knowledge—that you could possibly hope to meet.'*

Oz Clarke
British wine writer

*'Montes reds are highly respected in New Zealand for their quality and irresistible value. The Cabernet Sauvignons, Merlots and Malbecs are impressively warm and deep-flavoured, yet also vividly varietal, and the top Syrahs are of arresting quality. The cool-climate Sauvignon Blancs must also be giving Marlborough's winemakers a few sleepless nights.'*

Michael Cooper
New Zealand wine writer

*'I remember the beginnings of Discover Wine in 1988—four visionary men with a dream that implied great risks and enormous challenges. Today we see that dream transformed into Montes, a winery that produces some of the best quality wines of Chile. In 2004, Montes exported more than 400,000 cases of wine, whose high average price reflects both outstanding quality and their success worldwide—something we are all very proud of in Chile.*

*I still have my bottle of Montes Alpha M 1996, which I received at its launch many years ago, kept in its wooden box, wrapped in green paper printed with the now famous Montes angel. Ten years seems a long time to have resisted the temptation to open the bottle, but not much time for the tremendous success achieved by Montes and its three musketeers—Alfredo, Aurelio and Douglas.'*

Elizabeth Diaz
Manager of Viñas de Chile

*'Viña Montes is a combination of great vineyards, great cellars and great people... the result is great wines.'*

Hubrecht Duijker
Dutch wine writer

*'From a brave entrepreneurial start in 1988, Viña Montes has forged a reputation for producing world class wines from Chile. I was first introduced to the wines of Montes by Aurelio Montes in 1993, when visiting Hong Kong to judge an international Wine Competition. I was impressed by the wines, but also taken by the passion and enthusiasm Aurelio showed for his wines and for the future of the Chilean wine industry. Since then I have been fortunate to meet Aurelio many times, both in Chile and in Australia.*

*The strengths of Viña Montes are its pioneering spirit, vision and ability to innovate. I remember tasting a barrel sample of Syrah made from the first crop planted at the impressive Apalta vineyards, in Colchagua. Not only was the wine excellent, particularly from vines so young, but several years later, when I first visited the vineyard I could see the vision and appreciated the gamble of planting Syrah on the spectacularly steep slopes. Several vintages later, Apalta has now cemented a reputation for producing excellent Syrah, as Montes Folly has shown. Quality wine can only be produced from quality vineyards, and the new vineyard developments at Marchigüe and Apalta will underwrite future growth of premium wines. The wines of Montes are now available worldwide. This is in no small way due to the tireless efforts of Aurelio Montes and Douglas Murray, who have traveled as ambassadors for their company but also for the wines of Chile.'*

John Duval
Former Chief Winemaker of Penfolds, Australia

*'As a fellow Southern Hemisphere producer, Penfolds is delighted to have witnessed the unabated successes of Viña Montes over the last seventeen years. A Chilean champion of Syrah, via Montes Folly, certainly strikes an encouraging note here in South Australia. We respect the emphasis on quality—both in exceptional vineyards*

*and across a formidable and diverse range of wines, culminating in the lauded flagship, Montes Alpha M. The entrepreneurial and visionary style of the founding partners is well documented and recognised—true gentlemen in the world of wine!'*

Peter Gago
Penfolds Chief Winemaker, Australia

*' My mind goes back to the early 1980s, when I first met Douglas Murray. He was in charge of exports at Viña San Pedro and I the same at Concha y Toro. He was an extremely hard worker and traveller, a real believer in the quality potential of Chilean wine. When he and his partners decided to get together on the Montes project, I knew they had all the tools to succeed. In particular, two fundamentals: first, they were a group who shared a dream, a vision that they were capable of producing high quality wines and so break with the ethos that prevailed in the industry at the time. Second, each of them was more than talented—they were passionate. Vision and passion, these virtues are in my opinion the soul of Montes and the reason for its success.'*

Rafael Guilisasti
Vice-Chairman of Viña Concha y Toro, Chile

*' Montes Folly Syrah is of great importance for both Montes and the broader Chilean wine industry. It successfully shows that Chile is not simply reliant on a limited range of clean varietal wines produced under favourable (that is, easy) growing conditions and selling on world markets at highly competitive prices, but is capable of taking significant steps upwards. Hillside vineyards are expensive to establish and maintain in any part of the world, and the relative gap between the cost of river plain and hillside grapes in Chile is far greater than elsewhere. Nonetheless, the quality of the initial releases of Montes Folly Syrah makes one very confident about the future. The wines, after all, have been made from very young vines, and the quality of the grapes can only improve as the vines age. That the winery skills are there is beyond doubt; the Folly wines are very well crafted.'*

James Halliday
Australian wine writer and winemaker

*' When you have been closely linked to the development, teaching, production and selling of wines for 50 years, it is easy to see who has opened avenues for others to follow, who has inspired others. In the development of Chilean wine, Montes is clearly the success story. How does a Chilean winery achieve so much in quality terms and receive so much international recognition in a relatively short time? Because of the people behind it, whom*

*I have known for more than 30 years. Very few have followed their careers as closely as I have. Each of the four founders is incredibly gifted in a specific field and together they have been able to reach so much further than they ever imagined.'*

**Professor Emeritus Alejandro Hernandez**
Dean of the School of Oenology at the Catholic University of Chile
Former President of the Organisation Internationale de la Vigne et du Vin

*'For many years I have had a fascination with Montes—their dedication in the vineyard, winemaking skills and adroit promotion are almost unique in the wine business, and testimony to their fine management team. Montes has become the flagship of Chilean wines thanks to a perfect distribution network, impeccably managed by Douglas Murray.'*

**Christian Moueix**
Établissements Jean-Pierre Moueix, France

*'When I went to Chile in 1988 for the first time to study our investment in Los Vascos, I realized that amongst the large and historic wine companies there was a new venture called Discover Wine, run by two interesting characters, Aurelio Montes and Douglas Murray, who were travelling the world (as much as I was doing) explaining what Chile is about. I finally met them in the early 90s at a dinner in Singapore where, in the presence of the Chilean Ambassador, they were explaining Chile like nobody else could. Since then I have developed a tremendous respect for Aurelio, as leader of the new Chilean wine industry. We share the same long-term philosophy. He certainly knows how to make wines, talk about them, sell them ... and how to drink them with good friends like ...me!'*

**Christophe Salin**
Domaines Barons de Rothschild (Lafite), France

*'Over the last 18 years, Montes has arguably set the standard in Chile for site-specific grape growing, largely because of the visionary work undertaken by founding partners Aurelio Montes and Douglas Murray. Their innovative approach to the winery's traditional and non-traditional varietals has resulted in wines that never fail to impress. Montes wines are frequently the top-scorers in their class and have earned a secure place in the top echelon of the world's wines.'*

**Tom E. Smith**
Editor and Publisher of *Wine News*, USA

'The complementary characters behind Montes have created, in less than two decades, a wine company that has become one of the top five in Chile and one of the leading exporters of estate-produced wine. The Montes logo is an angel—indeed it was the Montes Angel, a miniature statuette of which Douglas Murray had given me, that helped me find my lost pair of reading glasses one Vinexpo. And after capturing the super-premium market with their brand Montes Alpha, the only wine to receive five stars in a recent Cabernet tasting at Decanter magazine, the partners have now released a new wine named, appropriately, Purple Angel. Made from the Carmenère grape, imported from Bordeaux in the mid 1800s and now unique to Chile, and a little Petit Verdot from vines high up on the hillsides of their Finca de Apalta vineyard in the Colchagua Valley, it continues the vision of the four founding partners to produce truly great, truly Chilean wine. Their country is right to be proud of them.'

Steven Spurrier
British wine writer and Consultant Editor of *Decanter* magazine

'All great wines, by definition, are capable of ageing and, in the ageing, of evolving into something more complex and sophisticated than the exuberance of their original youth. All great wines are also capable of travelling or more specifically, of staying undeterred and undiminished by the travel. Montes is one such effortless traveller. But a bottle of wine, no matter how fine or great, needs someone to launch it on its odyssey. Montes is infinitely fortunate to have in Douglas Murray such an able pilot who has tirelessly stewarded the wine into the waiting glasses of wine lovers across the four corners of the world.'

Ch'ng Poh Tiong
Publisher of the *Singapore Wine Review*

'I am always pleased to remember the Montes partners, especially Pedro Grand, from the early 1980s. It is admirable how Montes has developed in only a few years. They have selected great varietals from the best Curicó vineyards and have produced excellent wines, guided by Aurelio Montes' oenological know-how. Plus the extraordinary sales and marketing effort from Douglas Murray, who has travelled tirelessly through the USA, Europe, and elsewhere promoting their wines. Their record and success is there for all to see. It also represents success for Curicó Valley.'

Miguel A. Torres
Miguel Torres, Spain

*Santiago's landmark madonna, a gift of the French nation*

# *Chapter 1*

# PROLOGUE

'IT'S THE END of the line,' said a fellow traveller referring to the acres of empty seats surrounding us, as the 747 prepared to touch down for a bumpy night landing. It was 1987 and this was my first visit to Chile. At the tail-end of a long military government, the country was politically friendless and, it seemed to me that night, disconcertingly unvisited. Chile's wines were likewise virtually unknown— little more than curiosities to the world's wine drinkers. Watched by armed guards, we were a handful of arrivals who tramped across the floodlit tarmac to Santiago's old airport building.

I was visiting the country to learn about her wines and my Chilean host was wine marketeer Douglas Murray. With a true patriot's heart and unfailing enthusiasm Douglas was already broadcasting the potential of his country's wines, priming markets that were not yet ready to embrace what Chile had to offer. Amidst the indifferent offerings of most producers, Douglas's winemaker friend and colleague Aurelio Montes was making wines whose quality was opening up small chinks of international recognition. His newly bottled Cabernet Sauvignon, aged in then unheard-of imported French oak barriques, seemed to me to pull off an impressive sleight of winemaking hand. It showed the qualities both of youth and of maturity: structured, ripe and plump, yet soft in tannins and with a depth of flavours associated with older wine. Douglas and Aurelio embodied real ambition and winemaking potential. Together, they were on the cusp of turning a simple idea into a venture that, in a matter of years, was to help change the perception of Chile as a wine-producing country.

# HISTORY

The story of Montes is a small but significant chapter in the long and obscure history of winemaking in Chile, whose distant beginnings are entwined with the very founding of the country. Although relatively new to today's wine drinkers, Chile's winemaking goes back 450 years, making it one of the oldest of the 'New World' wine-producing countries. South America is a continent abundant in biodiversity, but it has no native vines. The first to grow in Chilean soil arrived in the baggage trains of the Spanish conquistadors, who arrived from the deserts in the north of the country. Vines were a must-have travel accessory for the colonizing invaders. Everywhere they settled, the conquerors planted European *Vitis vinifera*, ostensibly for the Eucharist, but with pleasures of the table no doubt in mind. No sooner had the breast-plated conquistador Pedro de Valdivia driven the imperial flag of Spain into the small hill that he named Santa Lucia, thus founding Santiago on the 12th of February 1541, than vines were planted in and around the remote new settlement. Wine has been part of the Chilean way of life ever since.

*A tree trunk constitutes probably the oldest winemaking artefact in Chile: the wine press located in the oasis town of Matilla on the desert route of the conquistadors. Dating from the early 1700s, it produced its last vintage in 1939. The earthen jars, or* tinajas, *are similar to those still used in parts of Spain*

The varietal mix from which colonialists made wine bears little resemblance to the international grape varieties now grown in Chile. The conquistadors brought with them the rustic País grape (known elsewhere as the Mission), which makes thin, acidic wine and is still grown in not insignificant quantities in Chile for cheap, local consumption. Other varieties grown in colonial Chile included the Moscatel de Alejandria, Moscatel Rosada (both still cultivated) and grapes long extinct, with names such as Aceituno and Huasco.

After nearly three centuries of isolation under Spanish control, Chile fought its way to independence in 1818. The new republic opened up to trade and new cultural links. Chile's aristocratic and mercantile elite, rich on the profits of mines and land, went to Europe on the Grand Tour and brought back contemporary fashions and tastes. Amongst the upper class, gentlemen began to wear the English frock coat, while ladies adopted the latest fashions from the salons of Paris. Afternoon tea-drinking became fashionable and so too did the enjoyment of imported French wines, particularly those from Bordeaux. Such cargo incurred high duties and it was only a matter of time before Chileans were asking why they themselves could not make wine as good as the claret they were shipping.

Chilean wine went through a rebirth in 1851 when the idea for change was taken up by enterprising landowner Don Silvestre Ochagavia, who introduced new varietal colour and winemaking methods to the country. He personally brought over cuttings of the vines that are familiar in Chile today from Bordeaux: Cabernet Sauvignon, Merlot, Malbec, Sauvignon Blanc and Semillon (plus some Riesling from Germany). He hired expertise in the shape of a French winemaker and so set in motion the beginnings of the modern Chilean wine industry. Ochagavia began a fashion that was followed by some of Chile's wealthiest families of the day, who set up wine businesses in the 1850s and 1860s. Attracted by the prestige of ownership of the equivalent of a Bordeaux château, they employed French knowledge and skills in planning and planting vineyards, designing wine buildings and making wine. Well into the 1980s, a significant number of these firms were still the prominent producers in Chile, and still in the hands of descendants of the founders.

The timing of Chile's import of predominantly French vines was to prove propitious, for within a few years the vineyards of France, and Europe as a whole, fell prey to the parasitical insect phylloxera. This root-eating, vine-killing microscopic louse originated in the USA. From 1863 to 1875 all the wine-producing countries of Europe became infected with phylloxera with catastrophic results. A cure was eventually found that involved grafting vines onto the roots of phylloxera-resistant

North American vine species. In the late 1870s, upon hearing of the disease's arrival in neighbouring Argentina, the government of Chile wisely banned the import of vines. The belief held by most is that phylloxera has never managed to surmount Chile's formidable natural barriers of mountain (the Andes), desert (the Atacama), ice (Antarctica) and ocean (the Pacific). A minority, however, believe that phylloxera has in fact made it into Chile, but that it has been thwarted by environmental conditions not to its liking. With multi-million-dollar wine and table-grape industries at stake, Chile takes no chances. Zero-tolerance rules ban the entry from outside of any form of vegetal matter without lengthy quarantine.

The last decades of the nineteenth century were boom years for Chilean producers. While Europeans languished in the wake of phylloxera, Chile, with its pre-phylloxera vines, partly filled the supply gap and flourished. Phylloxera refugees, particularly from Bordeaux, came with more technical expertise. Plantings grew, exports to Europe began in the 1870s and medals at international exhibitions followed.

But the early success of Chile's new wine industry was to be short lived. For most of the twentieth century, only the odd Chilean wine could be found in the dusty corners of the world's wine stores. So what happened to them for the best part of 85 years, until the likes of Montes appeared on the scene? Several factors contributed to the prolonged fading of Chile's star, which burnt bright as the nineteenth century came to a close. Europe recovered from the devastation wrought by phylloxera and the competition returned. From 1902 onwards, wine was taxed persistently and punitively by successive Chilean administrations. Then to cap it all, in 1938 a Prohibitionist ban on virtually all new vine plantings was slapped on all producers in response to dangerously high levels of wine and pisco brandy consumption. By the 1940s, Chile's wine production had come to a virtual standstill.

Furthermore, during World War II the Chilean government banned all foreign imports. In the absence of Chile's own manufacturing capacity, new winemaking equipment did not appear again until the 1960s, when import restrictions were lifted. With that came new viticultural techniques aimed at high-volume production, such as the *parronal* pergola training system from Argentina, which replaced the traditional Bordeaux-style low-trained vines, but with negative consequences for quality.

Worse was to come. Long-debated agrarian reform programmes began in the 1960s that broke up the *latifundios*, Chile's near-feudal estates (some of which dated back to conquistador Pedro de Valdivia's times). These changes were accelerated and radicalized, sometimes violently, under the Marxist regime of Salvador Allende. The result was the loss of vast areas of vineyard, social upheaval and economic chaos—hardly favourable conditions for winemakers. The consequent military regime of General Pinochet, which seized power in 1973, made Chile an outcast state in the eyes of the rest of the world, and the country's isolation lasted for more than a decade. In 1974 the ban on vine plantings was lifted, but this was of little benefit in a climate of political and economic difficulties, declining domestic wine consumption and non-existent exports. Many grape growers and producers were forced to uproot their vines or graft more profitable table grape vines onto existing roots.

It is not surprising therefore that when Chile emerged from isolation in 1989 after the Pinochet era, when the Montes story begins, its winemaking practices and habits were caught in a time warp. A free-market, export-orientated economy may have evolved, but winemaking equipment and habits had generally not. Yields from flood-irrigated *parronal*-trained vines were high. In the absence of imported oak, producers had resorted to Chilean beechwood, *rauli*, for cooperage, which did few favours for wine. White wines tended to be oxidized and stale, while reds were overstewed and tainted by unclean barrels. The big producers who dominated Chile's wine industry were making everyday wines on a large scale for an undemanding domestic market. There was a rudimentary appellation system to speak of but in effect producers could source wines from wherever they wanted and when it came to labelling, scant respect was paid to the integrity of each vintage.

The appearance of Montes was one of the first signs of an ambition to break away from the somewhat unadventurous, home-orientated ethos. This ambition would harness Chile's great natural potential for producing top quality wines, not for local pleasure but to capture the interest of wine drinkers in distant markets.

# GEOGRAPHY AND CLIMATE

Chile is the result of a colossal geological accident that took place some 60 million years ago. Two of the Earth's tectonic plates collided, throwing up the Andes mountain chain and a narrow littoral strip of land between it and the Pacific Ocean, 5,000 kilometres of which is now Chile. The country is a complete geography syllabus in one. Its deserts, altiplano, prehistoric forests, lakes, volcanoes, fjords, glaciers, ice floes and pampas are terrains so diverse and distant that they almost defy a sense of collective nationhood. In the middle of all this, by default, is a Mediterranean-type climate with conditions for growing vines that are considered some of the best in the world.

*Chile's picture postcard diversity: salt flats in the Atacama desert (opposite), fertile Central Valley (top left), southern lake district (top right) and Patagonian icebergs (bottom)*

The shape of Chile's landscape in the central fertile region is straightforward. Running north-south between the cordillera of Andes and the coast there lies the Central Valley. This fertile land of alluvial and glacial deposits and varied soils has been shaken dead-flat by Chile's constant seismic activity. Between the Central Valley and the sea runs a parallel broken chain of coastal hills, the Cordillera de la Costa, never more than 650 metres high and geologically much older than the Andes. Crossing the Central Valley and running to the coast is a series of east-west valleys, fed by short and fast-flowing rivers that form the basis of Chile's wine regions.

In response to pressure from the European Union, a new wine law was enacted in 1995 that tightened up Chile's denomination of origin rules, putting in place a system of regions and sub-regions. It stipulates that at least 75 per cent of a wine must come from a region or sub-region if stated on the label, and that if a single grape is named, at least 75 per cent of the wine comes from that grape. Grape varieties are prescribed but production methods are generally not.

Broadly speaking, Chile's wine regions are the wide east-west valleys that run from the Andes to the Pacific—geographical vertebrae that comprise Chile's spine. They do not reflect any intrinsic differences in terroir and their former climatic characterization based on north-south position has recently being overlaid by a more refined appreciation of east-west climatic differences within each valley. These are caused by the two overwhelming factors that dictate Chile's climate: the Andes mountains and the Humboldt current in the Pacific Ocean.

The Andes, whose ever-present heights rise up from the valley floor, act as a giant air-conditioning system from which cold air falls year-round, so that day-night temperature fluctuations are wide. The Humboldt current is a great mass-flow of chilled Antarctic water that curls up the whole length of the western seaboard of South America (making summer coastal bathing a bracing experience). The cool waters of the Humboldt exert a strong influence on the climate in central and northern Chile, cooling the coastal areas with sea-breezes and giving rise to the rain-free summers and bright, clear skies of intense luminosity. All these factors combined do good and useful things to vines, encouraging them to produce healthy, ripe and physiologically balanced fruit: grapes ideal for winemaking.

Chile is a small country in an immense landscape. Once described as 'the worst-located and worst-shaped country on the planet', until recently the sum of what the world at large knew about Chile was its peculiar geography (and its politics). Known for being the long thin country at the bottom of the world, that was where it stopped. If one asks what defines Chilean wines, the quip in reply is that wine, thanks to the endeavours of wine producers such as Montes, is increasingly defining Chile. Thinking wider, the great natural wonders of South America define the earthly power of the continent: the Amazon rainforest, the Andes mountains, the Atacama desert, the pampas, and at the very edge of the world, the fabled wilderness of Patagonia. Here are forces of nature, in the shadow of which man's endeavours take on a humility that gives rise to a belief in powers beyond the human; to magic and to angels.

*In the foothills of the Andes above Santiago*

# Chapter 2
# FOUR MEN AND AN IDEA

I N WINE CIRCLES, Viña Montes is almost as well known for its quadrilateral of four founding partners as it is for its line-up of award-winning wines. The personalities behind one of the country's newest and most innovative wine success stories are almost household names in Chile, so regularly do they appear in newspaper columns and glossy magazines.

Scores of new producers have appeared on Chile's wine landscape since the beginning of the 1990s. Many of these were initiatives derived from pre-existing business entities: grape growers or bulk wine producers who become bottlers, or high-profile joint-ventures between old firms and big-name foreign wine investors. Montes stands out because it was at the forefront of the recent wave of Chilean wine producers who make fine, 'premium-quality' wines. It also stands out because it began from

*From left to right: Pedro Grand, Aurelio Montes, Douglas Murray and Alfredo Vidaurre*

virtually nothing. There was no big money behind it, there were no premises, and each of the partners had to continue in other lines of work to make ends meet for a number of years while the fledgling business got going. Although other minority shareholders have joined the Montes board since the business started, historically the identity of Montes has been defined less by a corporate personality and more by the remarkably productive collaboration of four individuals. Montes was founded on the skills and knowledge—the intellectual capital—and the sheer commitment of its founders, and very little else.

Ask the four partners now what it was in their four-sided relationship that led to the success of Montes and what they can agree on is that it was often the absence of consensus in the boardroom. They were one winemaker, one marketeer, one financial brain and one viticultural engineer, each respecting the expertise of the others by not interfering in decision-making outside his sphere. As Aurelio puts it, 'If the founding partners had been four winemakers, it would have been a complete disaster'. So what are the founders' backgrounds and what brought them together?

# AURELIO

Aurelio Montes has always been interested in reaching high. As a schoolboy, he showed an early inclination towards altitude by representing his country in the pole vault. He loves to ski on the high pistes of the Andes. He has reached the peak of his profession, becoming one of Chile's most famous winemakers. And he is a real flying winemaker, taking to the skies as a qualified pilot. He often commutes by air to the various Montes vineyards 200 kilometres south of Santiago. His aviator's-eye view of the terrain offers him an advantage over other winemakers in the search for new vineyard sites. 'I love to fly alone and think about the landscape,' he says. 'The particular slope of a beautiful coastal valley will catch my eye as promising-looking for vines, with protection from the winds.'

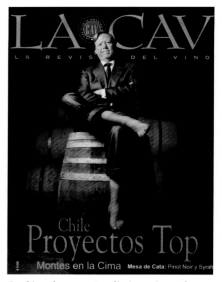

*Looking the part: Aurelio is a winemaker known for his sharp business sense*

Since his youth, Aurelio has been spurred on by the romanticism of heroic endeavour; by those who have achieved firsts. As a keen sailor he is inspired by Ferdinand Magellan, the first man to circumnavigate the globe (and rounding Cape Horn, the first European to set eyes on Chilean territory) and as an aviator, by the pioneering efforts of the Wright brothers. He also has his home-grown heroes. His maternal grandfather, Wilfred Baseden, was an English engineer who came to the north of Chile in the 1890s. Wilfred's brother, Clifford, was a World War I British Royal Air Force pilot. He was shot down while on a mission over France's Loire Valley, but he had the great fortune of falling directly into the gardens of the Château of Cheverny, subsequently marrying the owner's daughter, who had nursed him back to health. One of Aurelio's Anglo-French cousins, Yvonne Baseden, was a British wartime Special Operations Executive, who, aged 22, was air-dropped alone into enemy-occupied France and undertook perilous undercover work helping the French Resistance, for which she was awarded the British MBE and the French Croix de Guerre.

Another relation is Patrick Baseden, an exact contemporary of Aurelio and also an oenologist, former Deputy Managing Director of Veuve Clicquot Champagne and now owner of Château la Bienfaisance in Saint-Emilion, with whom Aurelio has made a wine called Sanctus, in so doing becoming the first to apply some Chilean know-how to winemaking in Bordeaux.

As I plan an interview with Aurelio at the London Wine Fair, I get a call from his office saying that Aurelio is not going to be able to come to London after all. He has to remain in Chile to receive another award and this time it's a big one, not for

*The San Rafael glacier in Chilean Patagonia (whose cliffs rise 60 metres) provides an icy backdrop to Aurelio and mate on the bows of his boat Folly II*

winemaking, but in the broader field of agriculture. In a country whose economy in the middle latitudes is predominantly agrarian, Chile rewards its successes in this field. The Salvador Izquierdo award is bestowed by the Sociedad Nacional de Agricultura, Chile's oldest and most respected professional association, for entrepreneurship in agriculture, and Aurelio is the first winemaker ever to win this prize. Although it is not a wine prize, Aurelio counts it as one of his highest accolades yet, an attitude stemming from his feel for land and the importance of agriculture to his country, one that goes back to his oenological education.

Aurelio's father worked in insurance and had no greater or lesser interest in wine than any other middle-class Chilean family. On Sundays, he would open a bottle of Cabernet Sauvignon, his favourite being from the old family firm of Viña Undurraga, to accompany the traditional Chilean dish of empanadas, or pasties. The family had a small house in the country at a place called El Monte,

*The mounted winemaker*

where summer holidays were spent riding, fishing and trekking. Although Aurelio grew up in the city, it was his love of the countryside that decided for him his choice of study at university: agronomy, the science of soils and crops.

Chile's education of its winemakers is unusually thorough. Students have to cover agronomy in general before advancing to oenology, the study of winemaking. As a measure of the success of Chile's wine industry, today oenology is the most popular of all the agricultural sciences at the leading Catholic University. Of all the science disciplines, it is the only one where student numbers now have to be

*'Aurelio is such a well-rounded person; he's a great oenologist, a great winemaker, and he always plays hard, whether it's golf, tennis, skiing or polo.'*

Alfredo on Aurelio

limited. But when Aurelio was an undergraduate in the late 1960s, oenology was an academic backwater, training winemakers in the methods of making wine destined for the basic 'garrafa' or carafe wine market. 'I chose agronomy because I loved the countryside. I was not setting out to be a winemaker,' says Aurelio, 'But I was looking for an alternative within agronomy, got good results in oenology, and plumped for it. But the teaching was very technical, with very little emphasis on style,' he remembers. 'There just wasn't the level of discussion and debate about wine that you find amongst students these days.' While his contemporaries were drinking rum-and-Coke, Aurelio was hooked on Cabernet.

Aurelio got an early and lucky chance to break away from the technocrat mould. His father must have been pleased when Aurelio was offered the job of winemaker at Undurraga, which he started the day after leaving university. Undurraga was one of only a handful of Chilean producers then aiming at better-than-average wines for the export market. It was a relatively small, family-run business and under the then Chairman, Alfonso Undurraga, Aurelio had carte blanche to experiment. It is telling that Aurelio was the first full-time winemaker ever to be employed by the firm. 'Before that, an elderly, part-time winemaker visited once a week and preached his never-varying recipe like a cardinal,' says Aurelio.

Undurraga was Aurelio's graduate school, where he could experiment with new techniques and styles and develop his own thesis on wine. 'They needed improvement to achieve export targets and I must have spoiled literally thousands of litres of wine during the process. But I learnt from my mistakes'. Undurraga was a producer that had significantly larger plantings of Riesling than other Chilean firms, the original stocks of which had been personally brought over from Germany by the company's founder in the nineteenth century. Aurelio was exposed to risk-taking and the progress that derives from it. 'Now that was scary,' he says, recalling the strategy of trialling an entire Riesling harvest with a previously unknown method of oxidizing the wine pre-fermentation, which Alfonso Undurraga had despatched him to Germany to learn about. Undurraga was Aurelio's opportunity to leave a still-isolated Chile to travel and learn from other wine-producing regions of the world, a chance that only a handful of other Chilean winemakers of his generation had. He became a great experimenter and during this time investigated new cooling devices and other winemaking gadgets. He was among the first in Chile to experiment with strains of artificial yeast, rather than relying on the vineyard's natural yeast populations, so giving more control over fermentation.

After 12 years at Undurraga, Aurelio suspected that unless he actually married an Undurraga his advancement in the firm would go no further. And he was ambitious. Alfredo Vidaurre was running Viña San Pedro, the second largest of the then 'big four' Chilean wineries (the other three were Viña Concha y Toro, Viña Santa Rita and Viña Santa Carolina). With 1,000 hectares of vineyards near Curicó, Chile's south-central winemaking heartland, four large processing plants and a sizeable chunk of the popular, domestic wine market, it was winemaking on an industrial scale and very different to the cosy world of Undurraga. Although daunted at the prospect, Aurelio accepted the post of Production Manager, and it was there that he met Douglas Murray.

*'What I admire in Aurelio is his talent to make wine and his intuition. He has succeeded twice now: at Apalta—an old pear plantation, and at Marchigüe—which originally looked like the Serengeti. He and I have supported each other; complementary in that sense, needing each other.'*

Douglas on Aurelio

# Douglas

Many valuable commodities have come out of the Atacama desert and Douglas Murray is one of them. From the bone-dry crusts and shimmering wastes of what they call Chile's northern soul came the minerals that created the country's wealthy mercantile class in the nineteenth century. Today copper, mainstay of the Chilean economy, is mined so heavily that extraction rates of its gargantuan open-pit mines directly influence prices on the world's metal markets. The driest desert on Earth produced the wealth of Chile's mining barons, many of whom became the founding fathers of an industry now producing Chile's greatest liquid assets, its wines. And in Douglas Murray, former Chairman of the government-backed promotional body Wines of Chile, and Montes' export director, the desert produced another wine catalyst.

But standing in Douglas Murray's office you might be forgiven for thinking that his trade is ethnic art, not wine. 'There's no more space at home and I haven't told my wife Lucy about all these yet…' he says rather coyly, referring to the contents of his room. It appears that this champion of Chilean wine exporting has been redressing the trade balance by some private importing of his own. Amidst piles of wine books and

*The Atacama desert: driest on Earth and Douglas's spiritual home*

Montes paraphernalia, wide-eyed wooden visages and painted totems stare at you from all sides. Douglas has a collection of ethnic art that must be unique in Chile, one that would justify a small museum (customs officials know his tastes quite well now after so many items have passed through). Half-elephant, half-man Ganesha idols from India decorate Montes' smart offices in Huechuraba, one of Santiago's shining new office developments. 'My Indian friends tell me it is the only 100 per cent good god, the others being ambivalent. Ganesha is the god of students and new starts and we feel akin to that,' says Douglas. 'It all started in the desert where I grew up. There wasn't much else other than Inca art and I became fascinated by it.' He started to collect when he first travelled on wine business to Africa and now knows where the best deals can be

*One of Douglas's pet interests is collecting sharks' jaws*

found in the world's antiques markets (such as London's Portobello Road) better than many locals. His artistic taste has been through various phases: African, Indian, Nepalese and Tibetan, Chinese, Aboriginal and, most recently, South Pacific Polynesian—a cultural gazetteer that mirrors some of the 70 countries in which Montes wines are now found.

The man who over the past 30 years of wine selling has spent on average seven months of the year away from home partly attributes his success in gaining the interest of importers to his interest in connecting with other cultures. 'I am interested in the spirit of places and people. When you understand their cultures and religions, you have a closer cultural communion and see that they put a lot of trust in their gods. And I respect them for that,' he says.

To trace Douglas's roots and account for his distinctly non-Hispanic name and looks, we go back to the early years of the twentieth century. The Atacama desert was supplying the newly industrialized world with the then basic ingredient of the agents of growth and destruction, fertilizer and gunpowder, in the form of mined mineral nitrates. The remote northern Chilean port of Iquique was one of the hubs of an industry in which the British had such a strong interest that it amounted to near-colonial control. From the 1870s onwards, vast nitrate fortunes were made on stock markets around the world from this outpost. (So much so that it attracted the interest of André Simon, founder of the International Wine and Food Society, and long-time sales rep of Pommery Gremo champagne. Simon travelled extensively around North and South America in the 1910s selling champagne; the story goes that he arrived at Iquique and there found a ready market in the desert port of very rich, very thirsty customers; after his sales tasting, head office at Rheims in France were nonplussed to receive a telegram from Simon advising them that the magnates of Iquique wanted to order Pommery's total production of champagne for the next vintage.)

It was to Iquique that Douglas's grandfather sailed from Scotland with his family in the 1910s, where he set up the 'Tienda Inglesa', a shop to supply the British community with goods from home. Douglas's father, who arrived in Chile as a small boy, later went into shipping and was posted farther down the desert coast to Chile's biggest mineral port, Antofagasta, where he met his Chilean/Italian wife and was eventually appointed British Honorary Consul. Douglas was born in Antofagasta in 1942.

Antofagasta in the 1940s and 1950s was a remote place to grow up. 'I am a product of the desert—it developed my character. Fresh water was a precious commodity and there were no excesses. You learnt how to be alone, how to persevere. As a boy, I used to go off and spend days at a time out in the desert on my own. The desert has its spirit,'

*Douglas on the edge of the world's biggest hole: the 800-metre-deep, 3.5-kilometre-wide Chuquicamata copper mine in the Atacama desert. The site has been a source of the metal since pre-Hispanic times and Douglas's Chilean grandfather developed the mine in the 1920s*

*'Douglas is lovable with a capital L. He has a way with people that you either have or you don't. Don't underestimate him—he devours information and when he says it's intuitive, you know in fact that it's well-backed with knowledge.'*

Alfredo on Douglas

says Douglas of these biblical-sounding experiences that in later life would stand him in good stead for solitary times away from home.

The invention in the 1920s of artificially produced fertilizer slowly killed off Chile's mineral nitrate business. The days when champagne flowed in the mining towns of the north were over. There was wine around but Douglas's father, being a true Scot, enjoyed his whisky. 'Tankers of bulk wine were trucked up the then dirt-track Pan-American Highway from Santiago, for bottling in local bodegas.' But this wine, which from the outset was rather oxidized, did not improve much from the hot, three-day road-trip across the desert.

*Douglas and Lucy on the desert coast at Chañaral in 1968, when they both worked in copper*

Perhaps unsurprisingly therefore, Douglas fell in love with wine not in Chile but elsewhere: Spain. His perpetual boyhood horizons of ocean and sand implanted an appetite for travel (apparently still not sated after 35 years of globetrotting). He decided to go to college in the USA, where he studied business and economics at Valdosta, Georgia. Missing his desert, he naturally returned there after graduating and started work for the Anaconda mine. That was in 1965; in 1970, the Marxist Salvador Allende was elected president of Chile. Having heard of the effects of that brand of socialism from some friends in Cuba, Douglas and his wife Lucy decided that the best thing was to leave Chile. Lucy's family were Spanish and it was either there or the USA. Lucy won the argument and Spain it was.

Douglas's first proper contact with wine was through the Spanish corporation Rumasa, a privately owned fiefdom of hundreds of businesses in the drinks, banking and construction worlds (later nationalized, then split up by the Spanish socialist government in 1983). Douglas worked as the export director for Rumasa and came into contact with wine through the business's sherry, Penedes and Rioja interests. The beauty of the sherry bodegas in Jerez and the picturesque old cellars of Paternina and

Bodegas Franco-Españolas captivated him. It was here too that he first appreciated the sensitivity needed for taking wine across cultures. He had as a visitor at the Paternina bodegas a supposedly expert and highly knowledgeable Japanese buyer. Douglas prepared for the visit by asking the cellar-keeper to line up a collection of rare, old vintages of Rioja for the special visitor to taste. Presented with the dozen or so wines, the visitor looked blankly at Douglas and then, without a word, proceeded to knock back a glassful of each wine in rapid succession. The cellar-keeper did not speak to Douglas for six months.

It was Rumasa that brought Douglas and his young family back to Chile. In 1980, it entered into a joint venture with a Chilean banking conglomerate called the BHC group. Together, Rumasa and BHC bought Viña San Pedro and Douglas became export manager. But returning to Chile was something of a business culture shock. 'When I arrived back in Chile from Spain, it was like returning to the country of the blind,' says Douglas. 'Wine exports from Chile outside South America were practically non-existent.' And at San Pedro they were in a sorry state. 'There was one order on the export books, just one, and we didn't even have labels to bottle the wine.' Douglas had his work cut out; but it was through San Pedro that he would meet Alfredo and Aurelio.

# ALFREDO

'I really enjoy solving knotty financial problems,' says Alfredo Vidaurre, Montes' financial brain. 'My methods don't amount to much. I sleep with paper and pencil next to my bed, so that when I wake up at night bothered by a financial conundrum, I can jot it down straight away. The next day, I find the problem is half-solved already.' Alfredo met Douglas and Aurelio at Viña San Pedro under circumstances that were not entirely auspicious. His introduction to wine was the task of rescuing the ailing producer and saving it from near-bankruptcy.

Alfredo is from a family that can trace its ancestry back to the Spanish conquest. His father was a senior official in the Post Office and his uncle was a cardinal. Wearing his characteristic pin-stripe suit, Alfredo sits in front of his roll-top desk and recalls in perfect mid-Atlantic English the long afternoons he

*Alfredo has a collection of vehicles that includes this 1957 Chevrolet pickup, in full Montes livery, used to ferry visitors*

*'We almost never see eye to eye, but I trust him implicitly. He would act against his own interests if need be—there aren't many like that.'*

Douglas on Alfredo

spent on the cricket outfield at his British school in Santiago. 'My mother liked to say she had two only-children, there being 18 years between me and my elder brother. She was determined not to pamper me and so she sent me to one of the British schools here,' he says. The discipline clearly worked, as Alfredo went on to a precocious academic career. By giving lectures and private classes himself, he paid his own way through university, where he studied business administration and economics. He then won a two-year Rockefeller Foundation scholarship to the University of Chicago, a popular destination for Chile's top economics students at the time (a group of whom, known as the 'Chicago Boys', steered Chile's economic reforms of the 1970s, influenced by the free-market evangelizing of Chicago's Professor Milton Friedman). Obliged by the terms of his scholarship to return to teaching at the Catholic University, Alfredo's academic career culminated in him becoming the youngest ever Dean of the Faculty of Business Administration and Management at the astonishingly young age of 29.

Chile cannot have been the easiest of environments in which to teach business after the election in 1970 of President Allende. 'It was not so much socialism, as all-out class war,' Alfredo says. 'The School of Management at the University was on a site away from the main campus, which the Marxists took over. Students at the School took a rather different view from the Marxists and we had a virtual siege on our hands.' After three years of Allende government, Alfredo had had enough and decided to leave Chile with his family for Panama, where he worked for the Panamanian government as a business adviser, mostly on public project evaluation. Four weeks later, the Pinochet military coup took place in Santiago.

After four years in Panama he returned to Chile and joined the banking group BHC as head of investments, which teamed up with Rumasa to buy Viña San Pedro.

# VIÑA SAN PEDRO

The early 1980s were financially unhealthy times for Chile. The world economy was in recession, and Chile's was in trouble. In 1982 alone, the country's gross national product dropped by a massive 13 per cent, a slump worse than any experienced during the Great Depression of the 1930s. A year later it fell a further three points.

Unemployment soared while consumer demand plummeted. In buying Viña San Pedro, Rumasa and the BHC group had taken on an inherently unstable business, which owed more than US$5 million in loans and debt. The rationale behind the joint purchase had been that Rumasa's expertise would lift the winemaking to international standard and BHC would provide banking know-how and soft loans at low rates. But they couldn't, because interest rates kept creeping up.

Things went from bad to worse and eventually the BHC group and Rumasa fell out, forcing the Rumasa staff back to Spain. Douglas, although back at home in Chile, was counted as one of the latter, and not wishing to return to Spain was therefore out of a job. The economic conditions in Chile came to a head when the Pinochet government decided to devalue the peso, after it had urged the transfer of debt into dollars. The whole banking system itself was bankrupt.

At Viña San Pedro, Aurelio's remit as head of production included the unlikely task of making whisky. Combining Scottish malt concentrate, Argentine grain alcohol and Chilean water, the firm produced a brand for domestic distribution. A visitor from the Scottish distillery Bowmore advises Alfredo and Aurelio in this 1985 photocall

Alfredo, who had been head of investment research at the BHC group, was sent in to troubleshoot at San Pedro. He was an academic used to analysis rather than management, but with the BHC group falling apart and nothing left to analyse, he willingly took up the task of saving the ailing producer. He had a job on his hands. Matters were so serious that the Chilean revenue service impounded all the company's assets to prevent them from being sold, because so much was owed in tax (US$11 million). 'They could have taken everything if they had wanted to. Taxes were being paid from a certain point on—it was back-tax that was the problem,' says Alfredo. He went to see the head of the Chilean revenue service, who told him 'My guns are loaded. My guns are pointing at you. But providing you continue to pay current taxes, I won't fire them'. Given the country's critically high level of unemployment at the time, any action that caused job losses at a high-profile employer of 2,000 people would have had political consequences. Fortunately, the guns were never fired. Nor did banks want to call in the debts, because they knew the revenue service had the upper hand. Under these tortuous conditions, San Pedro limped along, with just enough cash to pay day-to-day expenses.

Alfredo had to put a team together to achieve a turnaround. Firstly, he rehired Douglas to develop the export sales and bring in much-needed hard dollar currency. He then took on Aurelio from Undurraga as head of production and winemaker. But his recruitment happened under circumstances that were hardly encouraging. Out of the chaos that the Chilean banking system had been through, investigations had begun relating to embezzlement charges laid against Alfredo's former boss at the BHC group. Alfredo was caught in the same net and, along with 20 other colleagues, found himself sent to prison, pending the outcome of investigations. Three months later, he was released with his unimpeachable record intact. This surreal episode had seen Alfredo managing San Pedro from a jail cell, from where he recruited Aurelio. He could hardly have avoided giving a very warts-and-all description to Aurelio of the financial health of San Pedro. If it had not been for the intervention of Alfredo's wife and a mutual friend, who persuaded Aurelio that there were benefits in joining San Pedro, he might never have signed up. Winemakers tend to operate as a competitively collaborative group and Aurelio was also doing some consultancy work for other producers. He knew that his skills were transferable to another winery if need be; in addition, his old Professor from university, Alejandro Hernández, was one of the winemakers at San Pedro.

When asked about his financial whizz-kid reputation at Montes, Alfredo says ask any so-called whizz-kid about their success and they will tell you that it's all common sense. 'At Viña San Pedro we bought in around 80 per cent of our requirement for grapes and wine; 20 per cent we produced ourselves. The thing was to be able to buy grapes or wine on credit. Every winery did this then, but it was particularly difficult if you were a winery that was considered almost bankrupt. It took a lot of doing, believe me. I suppose getting closer to our suppliers and presenting an image of solvency—there was a kind of wizardry in that,' he says.

So there were Alfredo, Douglas and Aurelio working together with a handful of others on the San Pedro management team. The board of directors were non-operational bankers and not that interested in wine—just profits. 'We really had no-one to direct our prayers at,' says Alfredo. 'The company was in deep trouble and we were on our own. Against adversity it made for a very close-knit team.' (Afterwards nicknamed the 'Vietnam veterans'.) At one point, Alfredo wanted to take steps to raise the morale of the workforce. Aurelio suggested planting a not insubstantial 50 hectares of Merlot, in a visible location next to a main road near Curicó. Alfredo agreed in principle but, given there was simply no money available, did not see how it could be financed. Aurelio's plan was simple and low-cost: plant vine cuttings taken from an existing Merlot vineyard's pruning; there was no need to buy stakes and training wires, as shoots that young wouldn't need them for a year. The plan bought time and morale (and it turned out to be a very good vineyard).

Financially, the business was still on life support and eventually Alfredo was compelled to contact the state bank of Chile, Banco del Estado for help. He said that if they didn't assist, the revenue service would call in the debts owed, whereas if they put up fresh money Alfredo would be in a better position to negotiate, as there would be some money to pay the taxes. He heard nothing. In a last-ditch attempt, he sent faxes to the Ministers of Labour, of Agriculture, and of Economics, putting it plainly that Viña San Pedro had only enough money left for a few weeks; that there was the prospect of huge job losses; could they help? The Economics Minister telephoned and invited Alfredo over for a chat. On his arrival, Alfredo was surprised to find the head of the Banco del Estado waiting in the entrance lobby. The Minister asked Alfredo to explain the situation. He presented a solution to which the Banco del Estado assented: a debt-for-equity swap making Banco del Estado the majority shareholder. It gave the bank the right to appoint the Chairman of the new board of directors. But while San Pedro had found its salvation, Alfredo hadn't—he was promptly sacked by his new masters.

*The art and science of wine: in the lab at Viña San Pedro, Aurelio tastes his way through a collection of Cabernet Sauvignons*

For Aurelio and Douglas, their time together at Viña San Pedro was a perfect platform from which to develop their ideas; to explore export markets, find out what wine drinkers wanted and work on developing wines to match. It was they, the executive, not the board, that made the decisions; that planted the new vineyards; that opened up markets and determined the style of wines. In doing so they were laying the foundations for their own enterprise that was to follow.

Aurelio was able to continue the trials and experimentation that he had started at Undurraga. Changing the mindset and habits of the company was an enormous challenge, from the vineyard workers up to the assistant winemakers. His personal goal was to make better quality wines and yet Aurelio still had to produce the mass-market factory brands for local consumption. In a country of legendary fertility where the reduction of a harvest was antithetical to the notion of progress, Aurelio began to lower yields by bunch thinning, with the aim of producing more concentrated wines. He also knew the benefits that new oak could have in the ageing of red wines. Despite an abundance of timber in Chile (and a thriving logging business) Chile's indigenous oak is not suitable for wines. Viña San Pedro was the joint-first Chilean winery to import French oak barrels, from the top cooper Seguin-Moreau, that were used for ageing the best Cabernet, now a given for top wines (the consignment of barriques arrived in the same vessel as a batch for Viña Santa Rita). One of Aurelio's early achievements was a gold medal in 1985 at Vinexpo, the world's largest wine fair. But it was not for a Cabernet Sauvignon, as might be expected. The prize went to his cool-fermented Sauvignon Blanc. It was the first time that a Chilean winemaker has been awarded a gold at Vinexpo. And for it to be awarded for a white wine made it even more of an achievement.

In his eight years at Viña San Pedro, Douglas had taken the export sales from zero to 300,000 cases of wine. At first, money was needed in advance to buy the bottles and the labels. 'You can't get much worse than that,' he says. Despite politics-based resistance to Chilean wine (particularly trenchant in Europe) the world map hanging on the wall of his office became dotted with more and more little red pins: successful new markets.

Douglas and Aurelio became close friends at San Pedro and they began to share a common vision. The signs were promising. Even with high vineyard yields of up to 200 hectolitres per hectare and poor equipment, the basic quality of the wines was good. They also saw the early foreign investors beginning to show an interest in Chile; French too, none other indeed than Château Lafite, which invested in Viña Los Vascos. And with Aurelio's trials and yield reductions, they felt sure that a quantum leap in quality was achievable. One episode in particular was hugely confidence-boosting, and it came from the direction of the Napa Valley in California. In 1985, Chuck Wagner Junior of Caymus Vineyards, one of the most rated Cabernet producers in Napa, paid a visit to Chile looking for a supplier of wine for a second label called Liberty School. After visiting various producers, he was taken by Aurelio's reduced-yield, barrel-aged Cabernet, which would later be bottled under the newly-created Castillo de Molina label. A vintage was ordered and shipped to California (furthermore, the following year one went to an importer in Bordeaux). 'That was a significant moment, something of a turning point for us,' says Douglas. 'It was a real eye-opener. An indicator from a distant and quality-conscious market of the demands Chile could meet.'

The Viña San Pedro board of directors was concerned that Aurelio and Douglas were spending too much time on distractions and not paying enough attention to wines at the basic level. The wine employment culture was different in those days and there was no room for such a thing as a star winemaker who could determine direction. Against the backdrop of Aurelio's and Douglas's frustration and the clash of cultural objectives with the board of directors, it was only a matter of time before the two of them began to ferment their own plans.

Aurelio clearly remembers the day he walked into his office, closed the door behind him, sat down and set out his dream on a simple spreadsheet. The world's wine-drinking patterns were changing and consumers were drinking less, but better, wine. He put together a rudimentary plan for a type of wine business new to Chile, one modelled on the single-estate concept; not making factory-brands, only limited quantities of top-quality 'premium' wine for export. Aurelio asked Douglas in and straight away he had a partner. They knew that no

*Chile's gentlemen (and ladies) of wine: the* Cofradia del Mérito Vitivinícola

*In the early 1990s, Chile's wine leaders created their own brotherhood. The* Cofradia *is an elite and influential group dedicated to furthering the cause of Chilean wine. Membership is either automatic for those voted Chile's Winemaker of the Year or by invitation, occasionally extended to non-winemakers. Aurelio is a member by virtue of election by his peers as Winemaker of the Year in 1995. Douglas was presented with his poncho and hat in 2002. The* Cofradia *honoured Chile's son of poetry, Pablo Neruda, with posthumous membership, in recognition of the Nobel Prizewinner's love of wine*

bank would lend against them and they had to seek funding from a private backer. The obvious choice was Alfredo, whom they thought had money. It was at a black-tie charity dinner that Aurelio cornered him and spelt out what their plan was. Alfredo's reaction was swift: 'I'll buy into the project. I love the team. I'll go with you. So what about a winery?' Building one was simply out of the question, because there were insufficient funds. Aurelio knew that amongst his many contacts he would be able to turn to someone. He invited a couple of grower-producers into the partnership, and to their eternal regrets they both turned the offer down. There was, however, another character whom they all knew in varying degrees, Pedro Grand.

# PEDRO

Pedro Grand's family has been growing grapes and making wine near Curicó for more than half a century. But you would never have seen their name on a wine label. That is because Pedro was, and still is, one of the many growers who far outnumber the bottlers in Chile. They supply other wineries with grapes, or indeed wine, as part of an established tradition.

Pedro's ancestry is Franco-Italian, his engineer great-grandfather having left France in the early 1860s to work for the company that constructed the Santiago to Valparaíso railway. His Italian grandmother was a harpist who settled in Chile in 1910. So like many winemakers, Pedro is part-scientist, part-artist.

The outcome of World War II indirectly determined that the Grand family became vineyard owners. Pedro's father had originally been a banker, working for the Chilean office of an Italian bank. After the war, the Americans exerted their influence and forced the bank's closure. Pedro's father made the career move into viticulture by buying up vineyards near Curicó. He and later his son were obviously good at it, because the Grand vineyards commanded some of the best prices for grapes and wine, with many of the leading firms knocking on their door for supplies, including Viña San Pedro.

Encouraged by his father, Pedro went to learn his trade and connect with his French roots at the University of Montpellier in France, one of the world's pre-eminent nurseries of wine talent. He returned home in the mid-1950s, bursting with winemaking knowledge and technical know-how, but utterly frustrated at the backward state of the country's winemaking infrastructure: difficult-to-clean iron equipment, old cloth filters, and vats made from *rauli*, a native beech. His mission ever since has been innovation in the winery, travelling abroad and bringing back the latest ideas in winemaking hardware, from hydraulic German presses to state-of-the-art

*'Pedro is an outstanding engineer by default; he sees the future, anticipates change and prepares facilities in the winery. The fact is, every time he constructs a building or buys a new tank, we argue. Pedro carries on and, inevitably, I realize I was wrong. For example, he was right about constructing an isolated room for wines undergoing malolactic fermentation and for double-thickness jackets for cooling the tanks.'*

Aurelio on Pedro

bottling lines from Italy. 'If I had to single out someone who inspired me the most it would be the Spanish winemaker Miguel Torres, the man who brought stainless steel to Chile in the late 1970s. He has been my source of enthusiasm and inspiration,' says Pedro.

Thousands of kilometres from the service engineers and spare parts of the world's winemaking equipment manufacturers, Pedro developed self-reliance. He became a great technician, with a natural gift for understanding winemaking apparatus. In a country where all winery machinery is imported and engineers are not close at hand to advise, it has been a huge advantage for Montes having Pedro's expertise. Rumour has it he can disassemble a bottling line and put it back together having thrown the instruction manual away.

Pedro is an accomplished woodworker who has recently applied his love of craft and technology to his new Modernist mansion. This replaced the colonial-style Grand homestead which, made of wood, was being eaten away by termites. Large wooden doors throughout the new house are his own work, and he joined forces with one of Chile's telecom companies to create South America's first 'intelligent' house, in which all the functional elements can be controlled online from afar.

*Pedro in the cellar of his 'intelligent' house at Curicó*

With his vision for the new wine business uppermost in his mind, Aurelio called Pedro and invited him for dinner at his small house in Molina near Curicó to talk over the plans. But Pedro was hesitant, and it was only after his secretary urged him to take up the offer of a meeting that he met up with his future business partner. Aurelio outlined the plan and explained the need to rent part of a winery to make the wine. Pedro's reaction was immediate. He wanted none of that. He wanted in on the venture.

Aurelio's original business plan was beginning to take proper shape. Grapes would come from the small vineyard holdings that he owned, which amounted to about 30 hectares. Salaries were out of the question, so he would make the wine for nothing and continue his consultancy work. Douglas's input would be working on exports, also unpaid, for a number of years. Pedro's contribution would be the free use of his winery, Viña Los Nogales, up to a certain capacity, and the equipment there for producing and bottling the wine. Alfredo would put up the capital sum of just over 15 million pesos or 62,000 US dollars ('It was absolutely nothing,' he says). Target sales, ambitious at the time, were 50,000 cases to be reached by year five and the initial target markets would be the UK and USA.

Declaring its mission, the company's name was originally the inviting slogan 'Discover Wine'. This was later changed to the eponymous Montes, matching the name already on the labels and evoking the mountain imagery used in their designs. The partners met weekly on Monday evenings at Alfredo's house in Las Condes, Santiago's sylvan suburb. But Alfredo's stint in jail meant he was legally unable to officiate at the kitchen-table board meetings himself, so his wife Marisa nominally took the chair while the partners deliberated.

It was tough in the early stages. Although offered a seat on the board and potentially lucrative shares by the new banker owners of Viña San Pedro, Douglas was well aware of their asset-stripping rather than wine-improving intentions; so he resigned. He needed a source of income and was invited by Alfredo to join a ceramic tile producer called Recsa Cordillera, which he joined with his ever-loyal secretary from San Pedro, Sonia Montanares. He remained there for two demanding years while Discover Wine began.

Still with other work commitments to shoulder, in the early months all the partners worked into the small hours as Discover Wine took shape. Aurelio found the first year particularly stressful and remembers the dark clouds of mid-life crisis hanging over him. 'I was 39, I had five young children and I had no money. I used to wake up in the morning and feel quite desperate. That first year was very difficult but it brought me and my family closer together. I was particularly hard on myself and would prune the vineyards on my own as a form of punishment,' he remembers.

'We felt that there was music in the air, yet no-one else was hearing the music from the market. We felt everyone else was on the beach and we were swimming in the ocean waiting for the waves. We saw the wave coming, we swam and jumped on the board and we surfed it all the way. And we are still on it.'

From a simple vision shared by four men with very modest resources at their disposal, a form of alchemy took place that produced a range of wines that rapidly propelled Montes to the status of a 'first growth'.

*Apalta and the Tinguiririca river, Colchagua Valley*

# Chapter 3

# A FOOTPRINT ON EARTH:

## THE VINEYARDS

ALTHOUGH CREDITED WITH being one of Chile's most able practitioners in the winery, Aurelio Montes readily acknowledges that '80 per cent of a great wine is made in the vineyard, and 20 per cent in the winery'. His recognition of the importance of the vineyard contrasts with the perception of wine in Chile's domestic market that is still firmly based on producers' brands. Wine laws in Chile do not enshrine the notion of terroir to the extent that they do in the Old World. The rules allow you to plant pretty well what grape varieties you want, where you want, with few prescribed practices and no controls on yields. The only obligation on growers is to fill in forms for government statistics. But attitudes are changing, with producers looking for the country's best locations and associating wine—in export marketing at least—more closely with its geographical origins. New denominations of origin are being created, as the wine map is refined on the basis of smaller areas rather than broad administrative regions.

## MICAELA, CURICÓ VALLEY

The founding partners of Montes had come together via Viña San Pedro, and their former employer indirectly provided them with some of the vines to make the first Montes wines. By tradition, a nine-hectare parcel of historic Cabernet Sauvignon and Chardonnay vines at Micaela, south of Curicó, was owned by the head winemaker of Viña San Pedro; upon leaving the firm, the ex-incumbent would sell the vineyard onto his successor. No written record exists of when the Micaela

*A senior Cabernet vine in the Micaela vineyard*

vines were planted, but it is almost certain that they originated from cuttings brought over from France in 1865 by Viña San Pedro's founder. When Aurelio left the firm, his successor broke with tradition and declined the invitation to buy the centenarian vines.

In aiming to lower the yields and up the concentration of the must, Aurelio drastically changed Micaela's irrigation regime, knowing that the superannuated pensioners would have long-since developed root systems deep enough to find sufficient water. From one flood irrigation a month, their water ration was reduced to one a year. Older vines are generally considered to produce better quality wine and these *extra vieilles vignes* did indeed produce wine of a quality in linear proportion to their great age. Their historic status also provided the wines with an extra marketing edge for Douglas.

It is sad to relate that between the research for this book and its publication, the last of the Cabernet Sauvignon vines, which were perhaps some of the world's oldest at nearly 140 years, finally had to be grubbed up. Individual plants had begun to die in recent years, literally and unexplainably keeling over. Numbers in the antique vineyard population had been maintained by the old method of 'layering', a system of propagation only available to growers with phylloxera-free soils, whereby new canes from existing vines are trained along the ground and planted, eventually becoming new young vines. But the difference in yield and fruit of the young offspring created unwanted variation in quality. The Micaela vines' old age was testimony to the very long and productive life achievable by vines that grow on their own roots.

*At Micaela*

Montes has always bought grapes from growers as well as growing their own. In the early years and with limited funds, the four partners were well known enough in the wine industry that their personal credibility vouched for them more than any balance sheet could have done when negotiating with growers. 'Chile is a small country and people know each other,' Alfredo says. 'Starting with no cash and having to rely on reputation is actually something of an advantage in a small country. When we began, there was an oversupply of grapes, so it was much easier than if we were starting now.'

Montes still sources grapes from the Curicó area. In a commercially symbiotic arrangement, the company buys grapes from its own partners: from new vines at Micaela owned by Aurelio; from Pedro's vineyards at Los Nogales and from a further vineyard, Santa Marta de le Estancia, owned jointly by Pedro and Aurelio at nearby Rauco. Curicó is a relatively cool and humid wine growing area and the soils are fertile, producing what Aurelio calls 'good, honest wines'. 'Although pretty good, Curicó may not have the potential to produce Chile's best grapes, but with Aurelio's genius, he managed to make very good wines out of them,' says Alfredo. 'In the last two to three years we have decided to be even more selective regarding what we buy (even what we buy from our own partners) and we have been buying only some of the grapes produced in these three vineyards.'

Grape buying practices now have changed a lot from in the late 1980s. To obtain the quality that Aurelio knew was necessary for success, educating growers was needed. 'I knew we could do things far better than we were doing before, for example picking at the correct ripeness, and taking better care of the grapes. Simple things,' Aurelio says. At a time when the price of grapes in Chile was determined solely on their potential to produce alcohol (i.e. sugar content), he recalls coming up against the old-fashioned beliefs of peasant growers. Their winemaking was rooted in folklore rather than twentieth-century viticulture. 'Regardless of the grapes' maturity, for example, the date for the harvest would always be grandfather's birthday, or a holy day, simply because it always had been,' he says. Even today, the harvest time in less enlightened vineyards of Chile is still fixed without reference to the grapes' ripeness, but now it is the schedule of a transient workforce of pickers, rather than tradition, that determines when picking starts: grapes here one week; tomatoes there the next. Above all, Aurelio talks about the growers simply not believing in quality; there was no commitment to it, because the demands were not there. They used dirty, old vats that people were even very proud of (because grandfather had bought them). Entrenched ideas had to be removed that took a lot of time and effort.

Aurelio's strategy is never to become totally self-sufficient for grapes; he is happy to buy in around 30 per cent of requirements. Always on the lookout for new potential, Aurelio continually monitors the quality across different localities. As a consultant working up and down the country, he has an outstanding shop window to browse. When Montes started he could point to vineyards and say to growers: 'I want that parcel of vines…plus that one…and that one'. He knew the quality of the different lots and could cherry-pick the best grapes.

*Bathed in pearly coastal light, young Sauvignon Blanc vines flutter in the sea-breeze at Leyda. Plastic sleeves protect the soft stems from rabbits*

These days, buying in grapes is not just a matter of going to market at the time of harvest. It is more like vineyard leasing from one harvest to the next, or for a set number of years. Inch-thick contracts with growers are very detailed and demanding, specifying how the vines are to be maintained down to the level of pruning, grape cluster size and the precisely measured daily amount of irrigation per vine. Contrary to the assumption that buying from growers inevitably means compromising on quality, weekly on-site inspections by Montes staff ensure that grapes are cultivated to a standard, as if they were their own. As Chile's regions have developed their own reputations, contract prices for grapes from the top areas and their growers command the highest prices.

Montes also currently has long-term contracts with growers in Casablanca and Leyda Valleys. Situated between Santiago and the port of Valparaíso, previously vine-less Casablanca was 'discovered' in the 1980s and is now one of the prime regions for white grape production, renowned for the quality of its Chardonnay and also its Pinot Noir. Montes considered buying their own land there, but decided against it because it was too far from their centre of operations at Curicó.

Leyda is the most recent Chilean location to make it onto the wine atlas. This coastal region located south of Casablanca is the most westerly vineyard area in Chile, and the only one from which you can see the sun set over the Pacific Ocean. Aurelio believes this new, cool-climate area has great potential for Sauvignon Blanc and Chardonnay, and in 2004 Montes entered into a 25-year leasing arrangement with a grower, planting 50 hectares.

## LA FINCA DE APALTA, COLCHAGUA VALLEY

Vines have been grown in the Colchagua Valley, 180 kilometres south of Santiago, since the time of the Spanish conquest. Long known as an area from which large producers sourced grapes in bulk from old family estates, it has risen to recent prominence as one of Chile's top red-wine regions. This is thanks to a number of internationally famous investors and wineries, including Montes, searching out new terroirs within.

*Looking south-east across the slopes of the La Finca de Apalta estate, towards the Colchagua valley. The foundations of the new Montes winery are visible on the right*

Running east to west, Colchagua is bounded by high hills, the Lomas de Pangalillo to the north and the Loma Grande to the south. From the Andes the Tinguiririca river winds its way westwards through the valley, broadening out across a flat-valley landscape of fruit fields, willows and poplars, so typical of central Chile. Colchagua has a warm climate and, because of the river influence, a high water table and fertile soils.

Colchagua is where Chile's new multi-million-dollar wine economy and the country's rural tradition meet. Old veranda-fronted adobe houses now share the landscape with architect-designed, emblematic wineries with visitor facilities. The picturesque colonial town of Santa Cruz, Colchagua's hub, is the scene of a traditional vintage festival after the harvest. Chile's version of the cowboy, the *huaso*, wearing large, spiky spurs and cloak slung over shoulder (something of a cliché elsewhere), here still authentically works the land on horseback. Ubiquitous brown road-signs indicate the Colchaguan producers that have contributed to Chile's first wine-tourism trail, the Ruta del Vino de Colchagua, complete with newly laid steam railway.

Within Chile's denomination of origin system, famous valleys such as the Maipo and Casablanca are given 'region' status. Colchagua, despite having achieved near-equal fame and distinction, is grouped with its immediate neighbour to the north, the Cachapoal valley, to form the topographically meaningless Rapel Valley region, highlighting both the DO system's liberal use of the term 'valley' and the need for it to catch up with Colchagua's reputation. As Aurelio says, 'Colchaguan producers have been shouting a lot and the result is recognition, much more so than neighbouring Cachapoal, which could have as much potential as Colchagua.'

Back in 1972, fresh out of college and in his first winemaking job at Viña Undurraga, Aurelio had been dispatched to the then unknown part of Colchagua called Apalta, to buy grapes from a local grower. Although described (in the Chilean way) as a valley, Apalta is more correctly a five-mile-wide crescent within the Pangalillo range of hills. At its back, the range's highest peak, Bucatalca, rises to 1,214 metres above sea level, from which tall spurs half—encircle an amphitheatre—like bowl of hillside that descends and flattens out onto the river plain.

Huasos, *familiar figures in Colchaguan wine country, at the rodeo*

On his first visit, Aurelio was struck by the sheer power of the open space, like a giant crucible focusing the clear Andean light, and he fell in love with the place. He sampled grapes on offer and was immediately impressed by what he tasted. 'Now here…is quality,' he remembers saying to himself. After that, he was able to sample and buy more Apalta grapes while at Viña San Pedro and became quietly convinced of the location's special qualities.

*Apalta's shape gives it a sense of purpose. The name is Mapuche Indian and provides a clue to the area's potential for winegrowing: it means 'poor soils'*

In the early 1990s the shape and dynamics at the top end of the Chilean wine-supply chain were changing. Many high-quality growers from whom Montes had bought grapes were now bottling and selling their own wine. Montes' sales were on the up and the demand for wine was almost causing a problem. The time had come for them, as a firm, to buy their own vineyard holdings.

Land around the company's then area of operations, Curicó, was not an option, simply because prices had risen to prohibitively high levels and there was no good, affordable land left. The still unrecognized area of Apalta, so long in the back of Aurelio's mind, was a much more viable option because no-one had even considered it. 'It took 20 years to be able to buy the piece of land at Apalta that I dreamt of,' he says. 'It was quite easy though, because no-one else was looking. No-one else believed in Apalta.' Although there was no competition, the question of how the land was to be bought had to be answered. The firm did not have enough money of its own and partners would have to buy the land themselves. Douglas, however, was unable to contribute any money of his own into the purchase, yet did not want his stake in Montes to be diluted by new investors. The solution was to set up a separate company to buy the site (which a few years later merged into Montes), owned by the three other partners and outsiders (one of whom was Martin Wright, Montes' British importer, making Apalta the first Anglo-Chilean vineyard venture).

The plot of land that Montes bought, which they called La Finca de Apalta, lies in the very centre of Apalta; an inner-crescent, within the larger outer one. Part and parcel of the 500-hectare plot was a sizeable chunk of the Bucatalca hill that rises behind the much smaller portion of flat valley fields. The conventional approach would have been to plant vines on land that had been planted before, the lower incline only. But Aurelio had higher ambitions. He wanted to plant up on

*Now the slope is cleared, Aurelio has to plan the vineyard*

the hillside, onto the slopes, the type of land that has been recognized as producing better quality wines since the time of the ancient Romans. In the course of Chile's 400 years of winemaking in the Central Valley, however, it had been neither necessary nor possible to plant on such slopes. Growing vines on the extensive, fertile and flood-irrigated flat of the valley floor was easier. Without the recent (and expensive) technology of piped drip-irrigation and given the dry summer climate, planting on hillsides was impossible.

To intentionally plant up into the slopes was a ground-breaking move. In the northern hemisphere's more marginal wine-growing latitudes, growers plant on hillsides to increase vines' exposure to the sun; to help the grapes ripen. In Apalta, where guaranteed summer sun never makes ripening a problem, Aurelio did not want to help the vines. He wanted to make life more difficult for them; to make them put their energies into reproductive, rather than vegetative growth. 'To get away from the fertile valley floor where they grow too easily and vigorously…and stress them a little,' he says.

The clearing of Apalta was an act of faith of Herculean proportions in unchartered viticultural territory. Whole swathes of forest and bush had to be uprooted and removed. Seven hundred lorry-loads of large granite boulders that littered the slopes had to be removed or buried. Hundreds of kilometres of irrigation pipes were laid and extensive channelling dug out. The whole operation cost a financially draining 40 per cent more than it would have done for a valley-floor vineyard. Montes was struggling financially and according to Aurelio 'The lack of money was the biggest drama. Every stone removed and each vine planted was a painful cost'.

More recently, a further 200 adjoining hectares were bought and now a total of 135 hectares are under vines. The remaining 565 hectares—even with Aurelio's ambition—remains unplantable. At 45° and more, the upper slopes of La Finca de Apalta are as steep as it is humanly possible to cultivate anything commercially without terracing. Even if they attempted to plant higher up the slopes, clearing it any further would be prohibited by the Chilean national forestry agency, CONAF. The hills behind the vineyards are a protected haven of biodiversity, habitat of more than 100 tree, shrub and flower species, many found only in Chile, through which a walkers' botanical trail now leads.

*Syrah vines give way to protected oaks and shrubs on the upper slopes of Apalta*

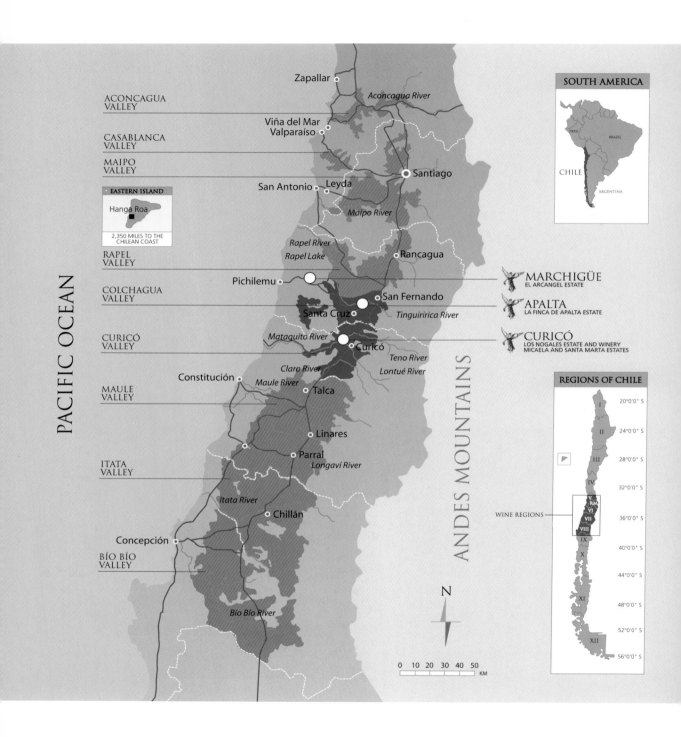

ACONCAGUA
VALLEY

Zapallar

*Aconcagua River*

CASABLANCA
VALLEY

Viña del Mar
Valparaíso

MAIPO
VALLEY

Santiago

EASTERN ISLAND

Hanga Roa

2,350 MILES TO THE
CHILEAN COAST

San Antonio    Leyda

*Maipo River*

RAPEL
VALLEY

*Rapel River*
*Rapel Lake*

Rancagua

COLCHAGUA
VALLEY

Pichilemu

San Fernando

MARCHIGÜE
EL ARCANGEL ESTATE

Santa Cruz

*Tinguiririca River*

APALTA
LA FINCA DE APALTA ESTATE

CURICÓ
VALLEY

*Mataquito River*

Curicó

CURICÓ
LOS NOGALES ESTATE AND WINERY
MICAELA AND SANTA MARTA ESTATES

*Teno River*
*Lontué River*

*Claro River*

Constitución

*Maule River*

Talca

MAULE
VALLEY

Linares

Parral

*Longaví River*

ITATA
VALLEY

*Itata River*

Chillán

Concepción

BÍO BÍO
VALLEY

*Bío Bío River*

PACIFIC OCEAN

ANDES MOUNTAINS

N

0  10  20  30  40  50
KM

SOUTH AMERICA

PERU          BRAZIL

CHILE

ARGENTINA

REGIONS OF CHILE

I                    20°0'0" S

II                   24°0'0" S

III                  28°0'0" S

IV                   32°0'0" S

V
RM
VI                   36°0'0" S
VII
VIII

WINE REGIONS

IX

X                    40°0'0" S

44°0'0" S

XI                   48°0'0" S

52°0'0" S

XII                  56°0'0" S

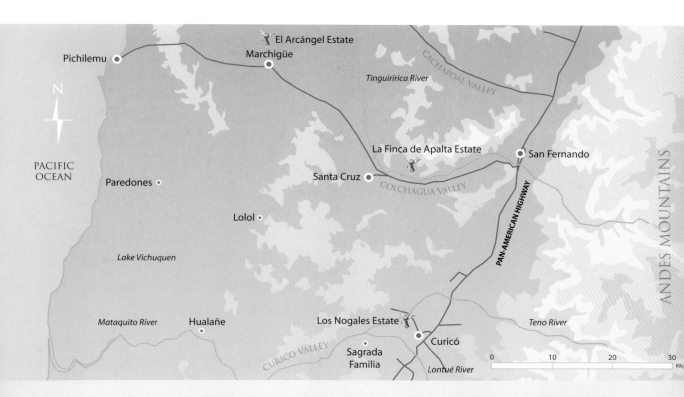

| | LA FINCA DE APALTA | EL ARCÁNGEL DE MARCHIGÜE | |
|---|---|---|---|
| Denomination of Origin: | Santa Cruz, Colchagua Valley | Marchigüe, Colchagua Valley | |
| Annual rainfall: | 750 mm (29.5 in) | 350 mm (13.7 in) | |
| Daily thermal amplitude: | 15° (30° to 15°) | 18° (30° to 12°) | |
| Degree days:* | 1,650 | 1,500 | |
| Altitude, above sea level: | 400 m (1,312 ft) rising to 500 m (1,640 ft) | 200 m (656 ft) | |
| | Hectares | | Total |
| Cabernet Sauvignon | 60.9 | 60.4 | 121.3 |
| Carmenère | 27.4 | 10.2 | 37.6 |
| Merlot | 13.5 | 12.4 | 25.9 |
| Cabernet Franc | 2.3 | 0 | 2.3 |
| Petit Verdot | 1.7 | 0 | 1.7 |
| Syrah | 16.7 | 43.9 | 60.6 |
| **Total** | **122.5** | **126.9** | **249.4** |

*Degree days are a measure of the number of hours that the temperature reaches 10° C or more. They are measured between September 1st until harvest time (end of April). A vineyard at 10° C or more will develop and mature well. Temperatures of less than 10° C may delay development.

## ∼ CARMENÈRE - THE FORGOTTEN GRAPE ∼

Much of what emerged from the pre-1990s time warp that was Chile's wine industry has been consigned to history proper. Something that emerged to restitution, however, was a long-'lost' grape variety, Carmenère.

In the nineteenth century, Carmenère was one of the constituent grape varieties in the Médoc blend, along with Cabernet Sauvignon, Merlot and Cabernet Franc. As such, it was brought over to Chile by the mid-nineteenth century pioneers. After phylloxera, the grape disappeared in Bordeaux, because when grafted its yields were too low. Carmenère days as a prominent Bordeaux grape were over and it is virtually absent there now.

Carmenère became forgotten in Bordeaux. Chile adopted the Bordeaux habit of growing different grape varieties in the same vineyard, and over time Carmenère became forgotten there too. Carmenère's cover was broken in the early 1990s. The government-backed institute Fundación Chile, which funds research on the country's natural resources, including wine, decided to employ the services of a French ampelographer to assess the quality of the country's vineyard stock. The conclusion was that much of what was considered Merlot was in fact Carmenère, long faded in the wine lexicon. For those who saw the Carmenère revelation as an immediate opportunity, the answer was to start bottling 100 per cent Carmenères. Here, after all, was a grape variety that Chile could call its own. Here was an identity (although Carmenère is reported to be growing in limited quantities in northern Italy under the guise of Cabernet Franc). Other producers were more cautious. Carmenère is a soft, low-acid wine with a distinctive vegetal, spicy taste. When ripened under the Chilean sun and well-vinified, it produces a succulent mouthful, but opinion is divided about whether Carmenère has the all-round character to be the new 'signature' variety of Chile.

La Finca de Apalta, is made up of two contrasting soil types. The flatter part is clay-like, with a water table high enough—unusually in Chile—for no summer irrigation to be required at all. On the steep slopes, the soil is usefully poor and well-drained, comprising a top layer of reddish clay and sand (similar to the terra rossa of Barossa in Australia), under which lies 3 to 4 metres of granitic soil, and beneath that, rock. After the winter, a little spring water seeps out of the mountain, but after that the slopes would revert to dust without irrigation. Growing grapes in this territory is pure artefact.

Terracing of the steep slopes in the upper part of Apalta was ruled out on the grounds of cost and concerns that digging up and disturbing the soils would damage their qualities. In the early years, erosion of the steep slopes after winter rains was a problem, but allowing grass to grow between the rows of vines and the natural anchorage of the growing roots has solved this.

The planting at Apalta of the staple red Bordeaux varieties Cabernet Sauvignon, Merlot, Petit Verdot, Cabernet Franc, as well as Carmenère, was an obvious choice. So too was a high density of planting—to reduce plant vigour—of precisely 6,667 vines per hectare (compared to a Chilean norm of around 3,700). Colchagua is not without its growers who believe they can achieve results with white grapes and Montes trialled some hectares of Sauvignon Blanc in the beginning. 'Sauvignon Blanc is a grape that, for some reason, Chilean oenologists consider more of a challenge than other white varieties. But given the warmth

*Horse power, readily at hand in Chile's equine rural culture, is the best means of dragging away large stones that emerge from the soils of upper Apalta. Horses' other role in winter is grass grazing, in which they are joined by decorous alpacas (top), that also add characteristically Andean zoological interest*

of Apalta, the acidity levels were too low. Our results with it were poor. Apalta belongs to red grapes,' says Douglas.

*Irrigation pipes and young vines on recently cleared, uppermost slopes of Apalta*

But looking up at the newly cleared bare slopes and soils, Aurelio thought of another granite hillside, thousands of kilometres away on the other side of the world: Hermitage on the Northern Rhône, whose Syrah produces some of France's greatest wines. It occurred to him that the variety was worth trying on the steepest upper slopes. His reasoning was instinctive and simple: the grape was in fashion worldwide, the Australians had done well with it, and the terroir of the slopes of Apalta seemed right. Why not give it a go?' said Aurelio to his partners. Other producers considered it utter madness to plant an untried grape variety on virgin land. But applying their faith in the expertise of their colleague, and in a manner that defines the Montes spirit, his partners said: 'Fine. We trust your instinct. Go ahead'.

Up until 1993, Syrah was virtually non-existent in Chile. Ever mindful of the devastating effect that the phylloxera louse could have on its wine industry, Chile guards its isolation with stringent quarantine rules. If you want to introduce new vines, you have to be patient. Two years' isolation is necessary for any plant introduced into the country. To import new grape varieties, you have to source them from government-approved nurseries in France, California, Australia or South Africa which develop pure, virus-free clones. Aurelio is part-owner of one of Chile's few nurseries authorized to develop cuttings under tightly controlled, sterile conditions. In their first shipment of Syrah cuttings from France, eggs of red spider mite, one of the relatively few vineyard pests in Chile, were detected. The whole consignment of 5,000 plants had to be incinerated, uninsured. It was a disaster; but second time round they were successful. Before such new plant stocks were imported, the country's vines were all direct descendants of those brought from Europe in the 1850s. 'They had their own genetic problems and viruses. It was a useful range of vines, but we badly needed some varietal fresh air. We have been working hard on improving the strains,' says Aurelio.

Apalta has a microclimate of its own that Aurelio considers produces distinct finesse in the wines. To begin with, it faces south-west, counter to the norm in the southern hemisphere, where vineyards tend to face north to maximize exposure to the sun. A look across the broad Colchagua Valley to the ochre-coloured Loma Grande indicates what a difference the direction of orientation makes. Shielded by Bucatalca and the Pangalillo hills, the morning sun hits the vineyards of Apalta later than it does on the valley floor and sunset is an hour earlier, so reducing the hours of exposure to the vine burning sun.

The prevailing wind in Chile is a southerly that blows gently up the face of Apalta's slopes. A fortuitous break in the Cordillera de la Costa farther down the valley gives daytime sea breezes a clear run up the valley from the coast 60 kilometres away. This further tempers the high summer heat, prolonging the ripening period of the vines and increasing the ripeness of the grape tannins. The broad Tinguiririca river, no more than a quarter of mile away, exerts a strong influence too. In winter, when in spate with Andean snow melt, humidity is higher and this is blown into the vineyards, reducing the likelihood of frost to almost nil.

In 1993, what is now Montes' La Finca de Apalta was an unheard-of, scrubby hillside, on the lower slopes of which the previous owner (a local hardware store owner) grew a pear orchard. Since then, thanks to Montes and other wine producers who have subsequently bought and planted there, the whole area of Apalta has gained international fame and is one of the most talked-about red-wine-growing corners

of Chile. 'When we bought La Finca de Apalta, we paid 1,200 US dollars per hectare. It cost us around 11,400 dollars per hectare to clear and plant it. Today, if we wanted to sell it, the price tag would be more than 40,000 dollars,' says Alfredo, with a smile.

*One of a pair of English Victorian traction engines kept at Apalta (of a type commonly used for power in Chile till the 1950s) found by Alfredo in old sawmills of the Chilean lake district, and still in working order*

Within a short space of time, the vines that Montes planted at Apalta were producing fruit of a quality so good that Aurelio was able to produce what are now two of Chile's so-called 'icon' wines, beginning with the Bordeaux-blend Alpha M in 1996 and the outstanding Syrah Folly in 2000.

Apalta has proved itself, with still relatively young vines, as a world-class wine-growing area, yet ironically it is still not recognized in Chile's denomination of origin system. Wines produced from Apalta grapes still can only carry the DO Santa Cruz appellation, which counts for little. 'In time, Apalta may get its own DO,' says Douglas. 'In fact, I think it should go beyond that, with official recognition of "upper" and "lower" Apalta, given the water table.' Under the current system, Chilean DOs are determined by municipalities not vineyards. As the region's human population comprises only a couple of hamlets, it could be a while before 'DO Apalta' is seen on a label.

# El Arcángel de Marchigüe, Colchagua Valley

If Apalta was a bold vertical move onto the hillside (and one that precipitated a Chilean 'slope-rush' amongst other producers), then Montes' next land acquisition in 2001 was a longitudinal shift on the map into frontier land. Montes headed west for 50 kilometres, to beyond Colchagua's fertile central plains, to where its hillsides recede and the valley widens out into a totally different ecology.

This is Marchigüe, a weirdly open, almost lunar, rolling landscape—the name means both the place of wind and of witches in Mapuche. Beyond lies nothing between the Pacific Ocean 25 kilometres away except a small, unexpected range of coastal hills. The landscape feels very different to Apalta. In the rain shadow of the coastal hills, it is exceedingly dry, with only 350mm of rain falling during the year, compared to Apalta's 750. Acacia trees and large-limbed cacti dot the empty landscape of dry grassland. It looks more like Africa than an extension of fertile Colchagua. This does not feel like wine country and yet land values here have risen six-fold since Montes snapped up land in 2001 ('It was worth next to nothing,' comments Alfredo). By that time, Montes's continued sales growth required further vineyard acquisition, and Aurelio's consultancy work offered him a glimpse of Marchigüe's potential. He had been asked to help plant vineyards in the area for a land-owning Chilean senator. The first grapes were so good that Aurelio wanted to buy land in Marchigüe wholesale. 'We collected a huge amount of satellite data that told us a lot about a site, the soils, the fertility and variations in temperature,' says

*Marchigüe before irrigation and vines added colour*

Aurelio. 'But in the end, despite all this data, it's all about intuition when you decide to buy land for planting a vineyard.'

Aurelio was attracted by the undulating slopes and cooler conditions of Marchigüe, whose microclimate is affected by its close proximity to the sea and consequent strong coastal breezes. Unlike other Chilean producers who have gone south in search of cooler conditions, he preferred the idea of going west. In Marchigüe you have cooler conditions, but none of the problems of rot associated with Chile's wetter southern vineyards, wind being the best fungicide. Not wanting to over-stretch themselves, Montes invited Veramonte winery to join them in the purchase of this land. Agustín Huneeus (owner of Veramonte), a prominent Chilean viticulturalist (who ran Viña Concha y Toro for many years and then owned Quintessa vineyard in California), was by then a minor shareholder in and director of Montes. It was perhaps fear of the unknown that led Huneeus to pull out of the idea, and in the end another backer stepped in, José Antonio Garcés. Montes now owns a substantial 600-hectare estate in Marchigüe, which they named 'El Arcángel'.

*Vine planting on a confident scale at Marchigüe*

Precipitation in Marchigüe is too low for any form of farming other than of sheep, and now—with irrigation—vines. But finding the water was a problem. The Tinguiririca river is no longer a companion water supply in Marchigüe, it having veered off north to drain into Lake Rapel 30 kilometres to the north, in Cachapoal. So several wells 100 metres deep had to be sunk to source enough water for irrigation needs. Water collects in a pre-existing artificial lake that is currently being enlarged. It forms the picturesque focal point of the El Arcángel estate and doubles up as the course for an annual company barrel-raft race between teams of staff from Santiago, the fincas of Apalta and Marchigüe, and the

winery at Curicó. From the veranda of the waterside guest-house, views across the lake of acacia trees half-submerged in water and large cacti growing amongst the vines add to the strangeness of the place, giving it the surrealism of a Salvador Dali landscape.

*False start? Water sports on the lake at Marchigüe*

Planning the planting and irrigation of this unknown terrain was made easier by enlisting the help of soil specialists from the University of Talca, a renowned centre of oenology in the Maule Valley, 100 kilometres south of Marchigüe. They painstakingly

*Views of Marchigüe*

mapped out the entire 600-hectare estate and produced a chart of the different soil types shown by water-holding capacity. Aurelio's instinct for the suitability of the land was combined with this data. Decisions were then made about where to plant different grape varieties and their precise degree of irrigation, which varies from once a week for some parcels, to once in the season for others.

Marchigüe is still in something of an experimental state, yet despite its youth as a vine growing area in 2003 it had sub-region status conferred on it. The first Montes vines were planted in 2001 from which grapes were first harvested for wine in 2003. To have productive vines after two years is unusual and it hints at the quality potential that lies there once they come of age.

On the upper slopes, Cabernet Sauvignon, Syrah and Carmenère are planted. The rows of each variety are orientated according to the predominant breezes and exposure to the sun, optimizing the ventilation of the vines and the ripeness of each variety. The lower parts of the slopes are predominantly clay mixed with quartz and mica and Aurelio is particularly impressed by the performance of Merlot here. The combination of a mild coastal climate, clay soils and Merlot has, once again, got him thinking on classic French lines: Pomerol in Bordeaux. So five different French clones of Merlot are being trialled on the lower slopes in the hope that one of them might reach a comparable standard. The higher proportion of clay than at Apalta results, according to Aurelio, in the Marchigüe wines being the more 'muscular'. 'Apalta is the elegance, with candles and long dress. Marchigüe is the Schwarzenegger,' he says.

# VINEYARD MANAGEMENT

It is to Chilean wine producers' great advantage that their labour costs are relatively low (average per capita income is US$5,000), compared to those in Old and other New World countries. Even the larger estates can benefit from the quality of manual husbandry in the vineyard and still be commercially viable. Montes vineyards are entirely manually worked and harvested, with no mechanization. (And in any case, at Apalta the steepness of the upper slopes rules out mechanization, 'or anyone but acrobats,' Douglas says.)

In its drive for quality, Montes has reintroduced old vineyard management structures while maintaining a progressive and experimental viticultural philosophy. The vineyards of La Finca de Apalta and El Arcangel de Marchigüe are manned by a combined, permanent workforce of 150, swelling with local pickers at harvest time. Under the old system used, each vineyard is administratively divided into parcels of 8 to 10 hectares. As Aurelio puts it, the 'wisest men' are given one of these parcels each, with sole responsibility for its performance over the vine-growing year. The parcel manager has a group of vineyard staff under him and he operates quite independently of the overall vineyard managers. At the end of each harvest, he receives a bonus depending on how well his parcel delivers, but only in terms of overall vine health and grape quality. It would not be true to say that each parcel manager is paid more the lower the yield, but introducing this system 'helped change the mentality of rewarding high yields,' according to Douglas. 'It instills a strong sense of pride and the resulting fruit quality is testimony.'

*'We have a saying in Chile, ponerse la camiseta, which literally means "wearing one's shirt". Employees who have their company shirts on love their work and this enthusiasm pushes the company forward, regardless of its financial situation. Montes has this gift and to help preserve it and our original philosophy of always searching for excellence, I have given myself the title of "Guardian of the Spirit".*

Douglas

Montes employs an agronomist at each vineyard, Roberto Pizarro at Marchigüe and Eduardo Silva at Apalta, who look after the purely technical aspects of vineyard management. The vineyard year starts in April, with meetings and planning on general viticultural policy, such as the degree of pruning and the numbers of grape clusters per shoot. Every week throughout the year, Aurelio visits both vineyards, or 'farms' as he calls them, and has weekly meetings with the parcel managers and the agronomists to monitor the vineyards' progress. 'In the summertime, I eat the grapes like a bird,' he says.

In both vineyards, tradition holds sway in the way the vines are trained, with the double Guyot system, typical of Bordeaux, used for all varieties. 'When I left university,' says Aurelio, 'vines were trained in the Bordelais fashion. Later in the 1970s, under the influence of the University of California at Davis we then used the open-lyre trellis system and now the Scott Henry vertical double curtain is in fashion. But I believe in whatever way you obtain higher yields, the quality will suffer. We use traditional, proven systems.' During the summer, bunches of grapes are removed ('a green harvest') in order to keep the final yields down; this combined with parsimonious irrigation results

*Tending young vines*

in some very low yields from Apalta and Marchigüe , varying from as little as 2 tons per hectare to a maximum of 8 tons.

There is still much to learn about these new, young vineyards and Aurelio's philosophy is one of continual experimentation and discovery while the vines mature. Every year, trials are conducted on individual parcels of vines; grapes from each are vinified separately to see what effect variations in the area of leaf canopy, yields and irrigation have on different varieties.

The search for new vineyard sites carries on, yet Aurelio never claims to be the absolute first to plant vines in a particular spot. 'There is always a sign,' he says. 'It could be as simple as the pergola on a worker's house. Or the memories of local folk of a vineyard long gone, which once produced good grapes.' Of Chile's future vineyard potential, Aurelio says there are two directions to explore: towards the ocean and towards the Andean foothills. He believes both areas have wonderful soils and climates to explore: two different opportunities offering two new challenges.

*The cellar of the Apalta winery*

# Chapter 4
## WINES AND WINERIES

I F A WORD could sum up Aurelio's approach towards winemaking, it might be 'empirical'. His career as a winemaker has been characterized by an almost restless drive to experiment and observe, to develop a rolling thesis of wine of his own; not to follow others. This methodology applies to his lesser-known skills in the kitchen. 'Even when I am cooking at home, making stew or broth, as a principle I never follow recipes. I do it my way,' he says. His view, after more than 30 years of winemaking, is that 'normally, all winemaking trends are, frankly, rubbish. All you need are good grapes and care in the way you do things. I hate to follow trends'.

From the vineyard to the winery, the variables and dynamics of the processes of winemaking are studied in almost obsessive detail. 'Tomorrow, I will be tasting more than 40 different wines made from different parcels of vines at Apalta, analysing the effects of cold and hot maceration, and severe green harvesting versus high yields. We go down to the level of numbers of bunches of grapes per linear metre, and per hectare by each parcel of vines and how this affects the quality of the resultant wine. Others do things blindly. At Montes, we are more of a scientific team. I think we are an exception in that way'.

Aurelio now has the help of two assistant winemakers, and a team of ten assistant microbiologists and computer technicians, all of whom are graduates of the leading Catholic University. Victor Baeza, whom Aurelio met through the charitable body Fundación Chile, cut his winemaking teeth in the Pisco brandy vineyards of the north of Chile and now oversees winemaking operations at the Los Nogales

*The original Montes Cabernet Sauvignon label*

winery in Curicó. 'We receive many visitors and students every year. We talent-spot, and if we like someone, we invite them to come and join us,' says Aurelio.

How different this is from the early days, when Aurelio made the first Montes wines virtually single-handed; when he had to wait at the local printer's shop while the ink dried on the first Montes labels. However, the circumstances of the birth of the first Montes wines did mean that a degree of prudence was called for. His first wines were something of a vinous secret kept under wood. Montes, then named Discover Wine, was formally incorporated in November 1988, but the partners had been manoeuvering before then. While still employed by Viña San Pedro, Aurelio discretely and speculatively produced the 1987 vintage of Cabernet Sauvignon from grapes grown at his own vineyard in Micaela. Using Montes' start-up capital, he engaged local pickers and vinified the grapes at the Los Nogales bodega, where the Cabernet sat in a combination of 250 new and used French oak barrels, until a demand existed to bottle and label it. 'Rather like the original Penfold's Grange Hermitage in Australia, which was developed in secret by Max Schubert in the early 1950s,' says Douglas.

After the sum of his experiences at Viñas Undurraga and San Pedro, Aurelio knew what he was doing. For the first wines he had the simple, dual aim of greater concentration and greater fruitiness; expressing the inherent qualities of his old-vine Micaela material. 'I was making the wine that I wanted to make and that I felt sure the markets would welcome. Everything was there to make very good wine,' he says. 'We just grabbed it'. With the help of Pedro's own workforce, Aurelio took measures that today are taken for granted in Chile, but which at the time were still the exception rather than the rule. The removal of excess grape bunches (a 'green harvest') in the early part of the growing season and a reduction in irrigation ensured lower yields and smaller Cabernet berries. Their high skin-to-pulp ratio helped in obtaining good extract. Picking was at optimum ripeness and yields were at the desired low level of around 10 tons per hectare. Simple steps were taken such as picking in the cool of the early morning to preserve the freshness of the grapes and packing them in small, 15-kilo boxes to prevent damage in transport from field to winery. In the winery sub-standard bunches of grapes were removed prior to destemming. Cabernet was given extended maceration, before pressing, oak ageing and light filtering.

On his formula for making wine then and now he states, 'There is no recipe—it depends on the year. But the hallmark of our wines has always been that we pick the grapes when they are very ripe. In my view, the sin of over-ripeness is less than the sin of green grapes. A fully ripe grape will have fully ripe tannins, even if over-extracted'. Aurelio's prescription for making great wine is frustratingly unrevealing for the inquisitive observer: 'We do not over-process or manipulate the wines. We just leave them in barrel, taste them once a month and rack them a couple of times'.

Once bottled and revealed to the wider world, the 1987 Montes Cabernet Sauvignon was something of a revelation that made the critics take notice. English wine writer Hugh Johnson said of it: 'It is a remarkable wine, combining the sort of cool-climate grassy Cabernet bouquet and flavours you find in, for example, southern Victoria and Tasmania with a most seductive soft smoothness and ample vinosity. It will be fun to see how it develops (if there's any left!)'.

## ∼ THE ORIGIN OF THE ANGEL ∼

With historical echoes of Chile's nineteenth-century wine ascendancy, the Belle Epoque styling of the Montes Angel also evokes the magical realism of Latin America. Designed for the labels of the first Alpha wines by Douglas's cousin Claudia Silva, it has since evolved for application to all wines (except Folly) in the hands of designer son-in-law Ignacio Williamson. The Angel now graces all Montes bottles. Angel statues and figurines, all of them collected or commissioned by Douglas, are present on all Montes premises.

But the angel is far from being the polished product of a branding focus-group. Douglas arrived at the image after a personal journey, one that by extension includes the Montes project, that gives him belief in protection from above.

A life-long succession of close calls on his own mortality,

beginning in his youth with near-fatal marine diving accidents (after one of which he was officially pronounced missing, presumed dead) and more recently with two horrendous car crashes, convinces Douglas that his survival has gone from the realm of probability into that of angelic intervention.

For those disposed to believe in it, the Angel represents a real guardian spirit behind Montes' success. For the rest, it is a strong brand, and one that symbolizes a communal spirit amongst members of the Montes 'family'. For Johnny Chan, Montes' importer in China, it means 'all the trust and good faith of the Montes founders, the importers and the consumers. The Montes Angel symbolizes strength from a shared passion'.

# ALPHA CABERNET SAUVIGNON

If the first Montes wines began in the vineyard, then the flagship Montes Alpha Cabernet was an innovation that started in the winery as a characteristically flexible response to market feedback. Independently, Alex Guarachi in the USA and Martin Wright in Britain (then Montes' only two importers) converged on the notion of giving the Montes Cabernet extra time in new oak. The inherent high quality of the wine meant it was ready to take on the complexities and depth of flavours imparted by extended ageing in new oak barrels. The price-to-quality ratio of such an enriched Cabernet would be irresistible to wine drinkers, Alex and Martin both conjectured. They made suggestions; the response from Santiago was: 'We are working on something'.

What they were working on was leaving the best lots of the Montes 1987 Cabernet wine in new 225-litre French barriques for an additional six months. 'Buying in the new oak, with our initial capital tied up in the first Alpha Cabernet Sauvignon was slightly risky, and a great expense for us at the time. But boy, was it worth it!' says Alfredo. The extra time in oak had a brilliant effect and the result was a wonderfully rich, well-structured wine that perhaps more than any other symbolizes Montes' achievement and success. In the USA, this new wine began life as Montes 'Gran Reserva', an empty epithet in the Chilean context, where the law allows the description Gran Reserva to be applied to any wine, irrespective of quality. Instead, at the suggestion of Martin Wright, 'Alpha' was added as a prime qualifier to the eponymous Montes, to create a universally pronounceable—and memorable—name.

The Alpha Cabernet Sauvignon was the first of a new kind of Chilean wine—dubbed 'super-premium'—that traded off its higher cost with a new-found confidence, and above all with style. Internationally, it leveraged Montes into pole position for winning new enthusiasts for what Chile could produce. At its level, it has remained at the top of the game ever since.

In 1997, a decade after the first Montes vintage, a panel of judges under the auspices of Britain's *Wine* magazine, tasted 88 red wines from around the world from the 1987 vintage, including Montes Alpha Cabernet Sauvignon. In the 'Bordeaux styles' group, which included Châteaux Mouton-Rothschild, Haut-Brion and Pétrus (to name a few), the Alpha 'performed better than any other claret except Lynch-Bages'. Even though 1987 was a middling year for Bordeaux, the news came as a vindication for Aurelio and Douglas. It was another significant moment for them. 'We felt we had passed a test. We had been acknowledged for producing a wine that had the ability to age, along with the best,' says Douglas. A similar tasting of 1990 wines was conducted in 2000, at which the Alpha Cabernet performed even better than the 1987.

Until 1998, Alpha Cabernet was sourced predominantly from Aurelio's 100-year-old vines of his Micaela vineyard at Curicó (with the 25 per cent allowance of grapes from outside the Curicó region permitted by Chile's denomination of origin rules). From then on, the source of Cabernet grapes for the Alpha switched from Curicó to Apalta, as its hillside vines came of productive age. The change in origin was made seamlessly and quietly, although the markets could not but notice a change in wine style. Continuity of the brand overrode origin in the marketing of the wine. But with the varieties planted at Marchigüe now beginning to distinguish themselves, in the future it may be seen as a marketing advantage to highlight any future changes in the vineyard origins, rather than play them down.

Other red grape varieties that have achieved the quality that gains entry to the Alpha club are Merlot and a Syrah. The Merlot is predominantly from Apalta, with additional grapes sourced from Montes' El Arcangel estate at Marchigüe. Aurelio's opinion is that Merlot is in danger of 'becoming boring' and that it has been overplayed in Chile; that it needs special terroir to have real personality. That he has found it in Apalta is beyond doubt considering the numerous international accolades the Alpha Merlot has received. We await the Merlot from Marchigüe, where Aurelio believes the clay soils and maritime influence hold great promise for the grape. His instinct about the potential of Syrah at Apalta has been borne out by the remarkable success of the vines there; grapes harvested from the upper slopes produce what many consider the finest Syrah in Chile, Folly (see below). Syrah grapes from the lower slopes, with the addition of a small percentage of Cabernet Sauvignon, still make a highly rated wine that merits the Alpha label.

*The Apalta barrel store. Chile has an abundance of forest, but its own oak is no good for wine ('Its effect on wine is horrible,' says Aurelio). So imported French and American 225-litre oak barrels have been a necessary prop for the success of all ambitious Chilean wineries. Aurelio buys both, for use with whites and reds. Although it is considered second-best by some producers, he is a fan of American oak, and has used it for Syrah and for Carmenère. 'For the first and second uses, it is too aggressive,' Aurelio says. 'But after that, it can be fantastic. French oak is milder, and smoother to begin with.' Montes buys from the top four or five French coopers, such as Taransaud and Saury and is selective in the forests that they choose, the drying period the oak is given, the degree of toast and the grain of the wood. They also buy from an enterprising local cooper, Toneleria Nacional, that imports French oak and assembles* barricas *in Santiago*

# ALPHA M

By the mid 1990s, Aurelio was ready for a new challenge. The vines of Apalta were coming on stream and he knew the potential for quality beyond Alpha level lay within its hillside soils. He was also aware that other producers of premium and super-premium wine were also thinking higher thoughts too. In the absence of any official quality descriptors in Chile, 'ultra-premium' wines were now being planned. (One asks oneself, what superlatives are left?)

Whether it was an expectation-building ploy, a genuine struggle to think of a name, or both, the new venture went under the rather sinister title of Project X. Realizing this would not do for wine, the X turned into an M, which incidentally

MONTES ALPHA

M

2001

CHILEAN RED WINE

SANTA CRUZ
APALTA SINGLE ESTATE
HAND PICKED
GRAPES

stands for Murray ('You couldn't call a Chilean wine "Murray" for Heaven's sake!' says Douglas).

For Aurelio, the creation of the first M in 1996 was a different task compared to that of Alpha Cabernet; it was back to the vineyard rather than creation in the winery. He knew what he was looking for and was much more experienced. Those parcels of vines on the upper slopes that performed better than others were beginning to distinguish themselves; these areas of Apalta were born and groomed for success, each receiving their own yield limitations and leaf canopy management.

M is a typically Bordeaux Médoc blend of Cabernet Sauvignon (80 per cent), Cabernet Franc (5 per cent), Merlot (10 per cent) and Petit Verdot (5 per cent—and sometimes called just Verdot in Chile). Aurelio's assemblage is not of course the insurance policy against the vagaries of climate that it partly is in Bordeaux. What he has adopted is the combination of vines for its complexity. Cabernet Sauvignon provides the strong backbone of structure and tannins; the other varieties fill it in with their own characters: Cabernet Franc with fruit and fragrance, Merlot with softness, and Petit Verdot with a certain spiciness. M is about a combination and a concentration of fruit: for greater concentration a green harvest is carried out before and during the ripening period with resultant low yields of around 5 tons per hectare. After picking and destemming, the grapes pass through a rigorous quality control checkpoint, at which the substandard are individually weeded out by a team of workers.

Once in the crusher, 20 to 30 per cent of the juice is 'bled' away to intensify flavours by increasing the proportion of skin to pulp. Selected imported yeasts are generally used for the fermentation, although in some years Aurelio allows the grapes' natural yeasts to work on their own. 'Young winemakers are

*Concentration and nimble fingerwork are needed for the grape-by-grape triage of fruit destined to become Alpha M*

afraid of native yeasts because you tend to have difficult fermentations as a result. But great things in life are difficult to produce. If you want good wine, you have to take risks and you have to work harder. Easy winemaking gives you easy wine,' he says. After fermentation, a traditional-style long post-fermentation maceration lasts for two to three weeks. The wine then undergoes full malolactic fermentation to lower the acid level and develop further complexities of flavour. Rather than blend straight away, the wine, still divided up according to the original vineyard parcels, is then kept for 18 months in new oak barriques from the Allier region of France. The final piece of artistry behind M is the assemblage, the meticulous blending of up to 20 different wines by Aurelio and Victor Baeza. This takes place three months before bottling. Aurelio's aim with M is to produce a 'balanced and harmonious wine, not a big muscular wine'. Where M differs from comparative Bordeaux wines is its approachability even at a young age of two to three years. How do you make a wine that is ready for drinking when young,

*Meticulous attention to detail goes into the presentation, packaging and marketing of M, for which Douglas took the advice of Pierre Beuchet, his French importer and agent of some of France's top wine labels. The taperingly slender bottles are imported from France and lead capsules come from Germany. Bottles are individually hand-wrapped in paper before shipment in* rauli *wood boxes*

yet has the ability to age? The answer Aurelio gives is ripeness, not just in terms of sugars, but of the grapes' 'phenolics', the chemical compounds that make up the colouring pigments, tannins and flavourings.

## Syrah and Folly

Only two years after planting the upper, steepest slopes of Apalta with Syrah in 1998, Aurelio realized that he had something special on his hands. The grapes were full of promise. Aurelio takes up the story: 'When we planted Syrah I told Douglas, "I think that Syrah will be fantastic". Then after five years I said, "Douglas, I have made a mistake, the wine is outstanding"'. The opportunity was clearly there for making something of this. Douglas wondered if they should blend the wine. Aurelio was adamant that having discovered a patch of land—a terroir—that went so perfectly with Syrah, it would be criminal to mask it in a blend. They should take it to the market in its pure form. And so (as if by stumbling across it) the idea for Folly was born.

Syrah grapes from the lower Apalta slopes go into the Alpha Syrah wine, it itself lauded by the critics. Grapes grown in the steepest, highest part of the Apalta vineyards are destined only for Folly. As a wine, Folly could be said to be an exercise in wine concentration; it is almost essence of Syrah, so wonderfully deep is it in colour and rich in long flavours. It is an exercise that begins on the 45° slopes of upper Apalta, where the naturally reduced plant vigour and spare irrigation result in witheringly low yields of less than three tonnes per hectare. (Bear in mind that yields for Alpha wines average out at two times that figure.) Berries are smaller than their counterparts on the plain. The harvesting and winemaking process is similar to M: individual berry selection, juice bleeding before fermentation, extended maceration, and 18 months in new French oak before bottling without filtration.

It was of course the background to Folly that produced its name: the problems and cost of clearing and planting upper Apalta; the scepticism of others in Chile at the perceived madness of the undertaking; the difficulties of managing and harvesting vineyards on vertiginous inclines; the idea of embarking on a second, 'icon' wine after M—and a Syrah at that. The naming of the wine 'Folly' seemed like the only rational part of the whole venture.

## ∼ RALPH STEADMAN AND THE FOLLY LABELS ∼

Having created such a sensational wine, what was needed was a label to match it; something that would reflect the spirit of Folly. Ralph Steadman is a renowned British painter and illustrator. His splashy, pen-and-ink caricatures of beaky-nosed wine buffs dipping their nostrils into blood-red wine were the image of the Oddbins British wine stores for more than a decade. He travelled the world's wine regions extensively as part of the job and also owned a vineyard himself at his home in Kent, England. In 1991, the time came for him and his wife Anna to visit Chile. During that trip he inevitably met Douglas, who detected Steadman's jadedness at the prospect of being shown yet another collection of new stainless steel tanks. He suggested that they forego the well-trodden visitor path of Chile's fertile wine country and opt for something unique that Chile had to offer, the absolute antithesis: a trip to the Atacama. Douglas wanted to take the Steadmans and show them his desert. So from Santiago he

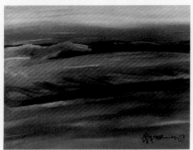

*Steadman's desert landscapes used for Folly*

drove them up Chile's aorta, the Pan-American Highway, through the browning landscape and shortening latitudes to his beloved hometown of Antofagasta, thence to the oasis village of San Pedro de Atacama. And back to Santiago: a mere 3,200-kilometre round trip.

It was an experience that Ralph talks about in reverential terms. 'Anna loves deserts, but I don't. I was afraid,' he recalls in his studio, one rainy winter's afternoon. 'We tore across so-called roads of sharp gravel in the middle of absolutely bloody nowhere. If we had broken down, God knows what would have happened to us. Only a desert man like Douglas could have timed our arrival back in Antofagasta just as all the tyres of the car burst, knowing they would not fail him'.

The hardy people of the Atacama, the strange lunar formations of its landscape and its eerie abandoned mining towns were to prove an unexpected inspiration for the British artist. He suddenly saw in the Atacama 'great variation, diversion, damage, twisted rocks… things happening'.

'I could not have been anything but influenced by it, so when I returned to England it blew me away and I sat and drew the paintings,' he says. The result was 12 beautifully coloured desertscape oils, each executed on handmade linen, which convey both the brutality and gentle intensity of the desert.

'The paintings would have sat in my drawer doing nothing unless I had showed them to Douglas during one of his visits, after which he had the idea of using them for Folly,' says Ralph. 'It was totally inspired. We could not have done better if we had tried. They convey the intrepid madness of the Spanish who crossed the desert to conquer the country, the same intrepid madness that drove Montes to clear and plant on the steep granite hillside of Apalta and produce Folly. It was such a happy chance that it would never have happened any other way. If they had said to me: "Do you want to draw the desert?" they would have got a horizon line, sand and blue sky above.'

Ralph criticizes what he sees as the 'tyranny of Bordeaux' in the design of wine labels and is delighted that his work has broken a mould. 'It was as brave to use those labels for a wine as it was for Aurelio to plant on those slopes. The madness of the Folly venture was like inventing a new art form itself,' says Ralph.

The Montes Angel herself was also subjected to Ralph's cartoonist wit. His fey, funny, tipsy-looking interpretation for the Folly label initially had chicken's feet. Douglas considered that a sacrilege too far, so Ralph shod her with working-men's boots for the Folly launch invitation.

And what landscapes will decorate bottles of Folly when the Atacama series is used up? Ralph's artistic compass has swung round to the south. For labels of the future, we await his impressions of a visit to the altogether different, but equally inspiring, peaks and wilderness of Patagonian Chile.

# PURPLE ANGEL

When in 1994 Carmenère made its re-appearance in Chile after decades of concealment, many producers jumped on the Carmenère bandwagon, keen to bottle what many were calling a 'signature' variety for the country. Aurelio's approach to the unmasked newcomer in their midst was more circumspect and he was not an immediate subscriber to the single-variety Carmenère fan club. 'It is a late ripener, and as a result tends to have low acidity and high pH,' he says. 'Its flavour can be overly vegetal and spicy and the wine it produces has unproven bottle-ageing potential. It needs to ripen fully but not overly so.' Before he released a Carmenère of his own, Aurelio wanted to spend time getting to grips with the variety and testing its parameters. 'I kept saying to those people who were practically demanding a Carmenère from me that I would let them know when I had made one that I was happy with,' he says. He wanted to find the right terroir for the grape and establish the best way to make a varietal Carmenère, before breaking away fully from the variety's historical role as a supporting grape. Not that he was averse to

fashioning Carmenère in a blend. Some 20 hectares of the variety had been planted on the lower slopes of Apalta, and its successful partnering with Apalta Cabernet Sauvignon has been demonstrated by the extremely moreish 70 per cent Cabernet /30 per cent Carmenère blend, bottled under the 'Limited Selection' label.

There were big risks in bottling a variety with unknown consumer appeal, and the markets needed to be approached diplomatically. 'I was afraid because people tasted Carmenère and said they loved it, but then they would choose a different wine,' says Aurelio. He took cask samples of Carmenère derived from Curicó, Casablanca, Alto Maipo (near Santiago) and parts of the Colchagua Valley to the USA and other key markets to gauge people's reaction to different regional styles. In the end, it was the Carmenère from different plots at Marchigüe that gave Aurelio the confidence he needed in the variety; the first full harvest in 2003 was vinified with extremely encouraging results. Marchigüe Carmenère is deep-purple, full-flavoured and resonant; the area's cooler climate suited the later ripening grape and gave the wine that extra acidity and bite that was needed. Coupled in equal measure with his rounder, riper and voluptuous Carmenère from the warmer slopes of Apalta, the result was superb. Although Aurelio could bottle single-estate wines from Marchigüe and Apalta—for all the varieties grown—he still likes the virtues of blending wines from the two areas under the DO Colchagua Valley, as the combination is 'outstanding' for him. His finishing touch to the intravarietal blend was the addition of eight per cent Petit Verdot. The percentage of the secondary wine is important. According to Aurelio, if you introduce more than ten per cent of a secondary wine into a blend, the unwanted character of that secondary wine will start to show through too strongly. Petit Verdot is a thick-skinned grape that punches above its weight with what

*The growing American and British fashion for rosé prompted Montes to create its first pink wine in 2005. Christened Cherub, it is made from Marchigüe Syrah, picked early for acidity, then allowed brief, overnight maceration for colour extraction. Ralph Steadman generously drew the label for a wine that was released with added poignancy. For the cherub on the label is named after Alfredo, whose health is in decline. The wine is dedicated to him by his fellow partners; Cherub honours the fraternal bond between them and the key role Alfredo has played in Montes' success.*

Aurelio describes as 'wild and aggressive' flavours; it is a seasoning grape that even in small doses can provide structure, tannins and extra colour.

Purple Hope was the rather diffident initial idea for the name of the wine that, after a protracted conception, took flight with confidence in 2005 as Purple Angel. Happy with the wine he has produced, Aurelio believes that Carmenère could be the flagship variety that Chile needs. But with the outstanding quality of Chile's new Syrah and its established renown for Cabernet, Carmenère still has something to prove before it supersedes them, and 'it could take a couple of generations for that to happen,' says Aurelio.

# WHITE WINES:
## SAUVIGNON BLANC AND ALPHA CHARDONNAY

Although Montes, like other Chilean producers, has developed its reputation chiefly by producing red wines, Aurelio's standing as a winemaker rests on a versatility that has also produced some world-class whites.

Aurelio's Vinexpo gold-medal-winning Sauvignon Blanc produced at Viña San Pedro in 1985 had demonstrated his adeptness at handling white grapes with limited technical resources at his disposal. Its great virtues were that it was a clean, crisp wine showing typical varietal character, the antithesis of Chilean taste at the time, attuned as it was to oxidized, yellow offerings. It was made in epoxy-lined cement vats with unsophisticated temperature control. He was on the right track. An early Montes Sauvignon Blanc was lauded in the UK's *Sunday Times* as 'a breakthrough and a bargain, a beautiful stylish, flinty, grassy-herby Sauvignon with a long Sancerre-like finish' and medal success continued with the 1990 Montes Sauvignon Blanc winning Aurelio's second gold at Vinexpo and Montes' first. A couple of years later, in 1992, Jan Read writing in Decanter described Montes white wines in general as 'outstanding', defying the odds in a year in which 40 per cent of Chile's crop was, unusually, destroyed by frost.

There was, however, one Sauvignon-related episode that almost put paid to all the partners' efforts and jeopardized the entire Montes project. Despite Aurelio's success with Sauvignon Blanc, and in the flurry of excitement that surrounded the reception of its wines, the firm accepted an offer of winemaking help. In the early 1990s 'flying winemakers' were making a name for themselves as hands-on seasonal consultants, imparting technical knowledge to New and Old World producers alike at vintage time. British importers Hedley Wright suggested that Montes ask the successful British flying winemaker Hugh Ryman to lend his capable hand and then bankable name to the 1993 Sauvignon Blanc harvest. The confident expectation was that sales of 40,000 cases would result from the collaboration, so short-term contracts were agreed with grape growers to meet the demand. The winemaker duly arrived for the harvest, but rather than the expected Hugh Ryman, an Australian colleague of his deputized. 'He made the wine, but then rejected the majority of the tanks,' says Aurelio. 'We only managed to sell around 7,000 cases in the end and the rest we had no choice but to sell as bulk wine at a huge loss.' To make matters worse, the grapes were bought in an expensive year. It was an unmitigated disaster. Creditors were at the door and Montes were literally hours away from bankruptcy. The land at Apalta was even offered to their neighbours, the wine producer Casa Lapostolle. At the last minute, the situation was saved by the rather reluctant acceptance of a new, fifth partner at the boardroom table: an investment fund, Estrella Americana, that injected life-saving capital in return for a stake in the business.

Montes' name needs no support for the trio of Sauvignons now produced. The cool conditions of Casablanca produce an expressive, well-balanced wine. A second from Curicó sees some oak and, with a view to the US market where the name and type of Sauvignon was first coined, is described as a Fumé Blanc. The third and most recent Sauvignon is from the coastal area of Leyda, first produced in 2005. What distinguishes this wine is its soft minerality; it is a wine that perhaps more than the other Montes whites speaks of terroir.

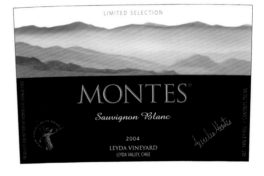

Montes' great achievement in white wines has been their Chardonnay. Mirroring the birth of Alpha Cabernet, the first Micaela-derived Chardonnay graduated from a 'Special Cuvée' to Alpha status in 1994, after Aurelio introduced barrel-fermentation and oak ageing. Montes Alpha Chardonnay is now sourced from growers in Casablanca Valley where the cool conditions and slow ripening produce low yields of 8 tons per hectare. This is a wine full of tropical fruit flavours and a complexity that improves in bottle. Eighty per cent of the Alpha Chardonnay is fermented and aged for 12 months in French oak barrels (of which 25 per cent are new and the remainder have been used for up to three previous vintages), with weekly stirrings or batonage of the lees to add extra flavours and complexity to the wine; the remaining 20 per cent sees its passage through stainless steel to act as a refreshing counterbalance in the final wine. Careful

choice of artificial yeasts from a broad range available from Europe is a must because, for whites, Aurelio never relies on wild yeasts; their numbers are too low in the 'clean', pressed juice and incomplete fermentations can result. There is partial malolactic fermentation, enough to create the buttery complexity associated with it, but not so much as to cause an imbalance in overall acidity level.

Montes' Late Harvest dessert wine deserves a glowing mention. Sweet pudding wines are not products that you immediately associate with Chile. Their output is limited and intermittent because Chile's vineyards are generally too dry for the development of the necessary agent in their production, botrytis mould. A Brussels ban on the wines—only recently lifted—is another reason why they are not better known in the European Union at least.

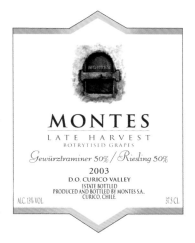

But at Curicó and in other southern wine areas, damp misty mornings and warm afternoons in the autumn month of June can, in some years, create the right conditions for the kindly form of botrytis that dries out the grapes, producing wines of intense extract and sweetness. Montes Late Harvest is a floral Gewürztraminer/Riesling blend from Curicó. The 1996 vintage surprised many when it scooped a Civart trophy at the Vinexpo of 1997, the exhibition's highest level of award, given to the best of the gold medal winners.

*In 2002, Montes announced the expansion of its operation into Mendoza, Argentina, a short hop across the Andean Cordillera. The Kaiken is a wild and hardy Patagonian goose and a frequent flyer over the Andes between Chile and Argentina. A winery is leased in the Vistalba region of Mendoza and grapes have been bought from 15 to 20 diverse growers, allowing Montes to determine the consistently best areas, especially those not prone to Mendoza's frosts and notorious summer showers of golf-ball hailstones. Seventy hectares of land have recently been purchased in Agrelo. Kaiken Cabernet Sauvignon and Malbec wines have already attracted international attention and awards*

# WINERIES

Before the construction of a new winery at Apalta, Montes had been one of Chile's foremost wine producers but did not own its own winery. Montes was, and remains, a tenant, with Pedro Grand as their landlord. His contribution in kind to the start-up capital of Montes was the free use of the space, vats, bottling line and manpower of his Los Nogales winery at Curicó. A functional old workhorse bodega of no great architectural beauty, it is of passing historical interest because of its nineteenth-century adobe (mud-brick) walls, that rendered it uninsurable against Chile's ever-present earthquake threat.

The deal between Montes and Pedro was that they had free use of his Los Nogales facilities up to what was considered an ambitious ceiling of 300,000 litres (33,333 cases). But sales during the first years of Montes' life were so buoyant that this ceiling was quickly and unexpectedly surpassed after the third vintage in 1990. A further leasing agreement was drawn up and Montes has been renting from Pedro ever since. A new extension to the old Los Nogales bodega now houses rows of stainless steel tanks with a total capacity of more than 7.5 million litres, some of which belong to Pedro and some to Montes.

*Pedro, Aurelio and Douglas at the entrance of the Los Nogales bodega*

Further growth has required yet more capacity. Extra winery space and equipment is leased from a bodega at Los Lirios near Rancagua, north of Curicó, as well as occasionally from other third parties on a yearly or seasonal basis. But until the construction of Montes' own winery at Apalta in 2004, Los Nogales was where the majority of Montes wines were made. (In the early days 'Nogales' was chosen as the name for some lower-priced wines. These were swiftly renamed 'Villa Montes' after someone tactfully pointed out that Los Nogales was the name of a town synonymous with low-life crime.)

Montes' policy of renting capacity avoided the need for capital-intensive projects. But in 2000 it was decided that an on-site winery should be built at Apalta, dedicated to the production and storage of Alpha M, Folly, Purple Angel and all

*Aurelio 'pumping over' fermenting Cabernet Sauvignon in the Los Nogales winery. The wine benefits from the momentary 'airing', before it is piped back to the layer of grape skins at the top of the tank for further extraction of colour and flavours*

Alpha Reds. It made practical sense to make these wines in situ rather than truck the grapes to the Curicó winery 50 kilometres away. From an image point of view, Montes' eminent standing as a producer and the 'iconic' status of its top wines required a winery to match, and one that would also cater for the increasing number of tourists in the Colchagua Valley. Montes had made their agricultural mark on Apalta. The time had come to make their architectural one.

This was Aurelio's opportunity to create a winery just as he wanted it. He and his winemaking team visited more than 20 producers in California's Napa Valley and in Australia before arriving at a vision of what was required, and a shopping list of expensive hardware. Heralded as 'state-of-the-art', much of what is in the new winery is, actually, distinctly revivalist and back-to-basics. Aurelio's firm belief in keeping the manipulation of wine to a minimum dictated that pumps would have no place in the new winery. Gravity, the most primitive force of them all, would move grapes, the must (i.e. the juice before and during fermentation) and new wine around the building. And although consigned to history by many winemakers, Aurelio wanted to bring back vertical basket presses rather than use the more contemporary horizontal press. The modern interpretation of the old wooden basket press, from Austrian-French makers Bücher-Vaslin, differs from its predecessors. It is made of stainless steel, is airtight and is controlled by microchips rather than muscle power, but the principle of gentle pressing remains the same. 'We are reverting to old practices, realizing that our forebears were doing things the correct way,' says Aurelio. 'I went to Napa to see new vertical presses in action and saw that their gentle pressing made a real difference to the resulting wine. The only drawback is their slow speed when you have high tonnage of grapes.' In addition to ubiquitous stainless steel tanks, ten relatively small 10,000-litre oak fermentation vats, nine imported from France and one made by the leading Chilean cooper Toneleria Nacional, are installed at Apalta.

The small size helps control what goes on inside them during fermentation, and each is equipped with refrigerant-containing immersion plates that can warm or cool the must. Aurelio says the wooden vats provide good thermal reaction and gas interaction. He can protect the wines against the autumnal drop in temperature that can occur in April and May during the harvest. Conversely, the temperature can be lowered if needed.

The partners engaged the services of Samuel Claro, of Chilean partnership Claro and Swinburn, as architect of the new bodega. He had already designed wineries for, amongst others, Viña Altair and Viña Errázuriz. The initial plan was to build the winery at the foot of the property by the access road to the vineyard. Plans faltered over finance and the project was put on hold for a couple of years. As an interim measure, a straightforward, air-conditioned above-ground

*Elderly 'Founders' Reserve' Cabernet Sauvignon vines transplanted from the Micaela vineyard front their retirement home, the new Apalta winery*

barrel store was built for the storage of cask wine destined for the two top labels of M and Folly and the Alpha reds. In 2002, work got underway again on the new winery. It was decided to move the location to the lower part of the vineyards, to enhance the view of the upper slopes and the perspective of the building from the edges of the estate. The high water table in the lower part of Apalta meant that digging an underground cellar was out of the question. So instead, earth was piled up around the flanks of the building to help create cool subterranean conditions above ground, which are enhanced with air conditioning on the inside.

Working with South African conceptual engineers Technique Trading, Samuel Claro's concept was a building that would blend in and pay architectural homage to its great natural surroundings as well as the processes of a winery, rather than make a grandiose statement of human intervention.

Before Claro's plans were finished, they were subjected to a dogma not normally associated with winery planning: feng shui. Douglas's experiences in the Far East have made him an ardent believer in the Chinese philosophy and at his behest, Chile's feng shui expert Sylvia Galleguillos was asked to come and dispense her wisdom. She had given the new Montes office in Santiago the feng shui OK after ordering the drilling of small interconnecting holes between various rooms, and Aurelio and Alfredo had come round to accepting Douglas's wish for feng shui to be applied to the new winery. She visited Apalta and at the spot judged to be the centre of the new winery, eucharistically transferred some Alpha Cabernet into 3,000-year-old Shang Dynasty ceremonial wine decanters, rang bells and said prayers for the success of the new building. Wine was then poured onto the soil to enhance its fertility and well-being and the remainder handed round for the assembled workers to sip.

At the entrance of the building, Claro's plan had included a walkway over a small lagoon, the water of which flowed away from the building. A fundamental tenet of feng shui is that prosperity will come only if water, which represents energy, flows towards the centre of a building rather than away from it. The direction of the flow was duly reversed. At the centre of the winery is a fountain beneath an iris-like skylight that represents the sun by day and the moon by night. According to feng shui, this is the point of distribution of energy, connecting the building to the universe and beyond.

*Seen from the slopes of Apalta, the half-buried winery sits discreetly, bunker-like on the vineyard plain. The rooftop reception and handling area for grapes is in full view*

The winery's position blends in with the gentle slope of the vineyard. Being gravity fed has turned some of the building's functionality on its head. Raised by forklift, the grapes are delivered to the roof, rather than to the ground floor of the building. In the open air, bunches are destemmed, faulty grapes individually rejected by hand, and the remainder gently pressed before dropping through chute-like openings in the roof floor leading to fermentation tanks below. The whole place revolves around gravitational logic. Because there are no pumps, a giant lift was built (the first such contraption in Chile) that can raise whole tanks of wine up from the ground level to the floor above.

*Crossing the entrance lagoon of the new winery*

*Inside the new Apalta winery. The wine elevator is on the right*

*The local priest blesses the winery in front of assembled importers and friends and (right) traditional folk dancing at the formal opening of the Apalta winery*

The US$6.5 million cost of the new winery was paid for by Montes' own reserves and bank credit, the majority being the latter. 'We have been very fortunate because the interest rate for bank financing has never been as low as it is today, at least during my lifetime,' says Alfredo. Despite the low cost of credit, the weakening US dollar (in which Montes sells its wines) has put a hold on the full completion of the project.

Viewed from above, Claro's plan for the building resembles a knotted bow tie, and so far only the left-hand bow and central knot have been constructed. The right-hand side, which was to be used for storage, remains unbuilt. But this does not appear to have upset the feng-shui energy-balance in the building, judging by the quality of the wines emerging, nor the high-spirited celebrations of the grand opening. In front of assembled importers, press and friends, the local priest first blessed the new plant, after which a ribbon was cut jointly by Aurelio, Douglas and Alfredo. A folkloric troupe performed Chile's national dance, the *cueca*, and a young ballerina danced the part of the Montes angel.

Even with the opening of the new Apalta winery, the problem of ever-increasing capacity needs has not been solved. The leasing arrangement with Pedro is up for renegotiation at the end of 2006. And even if the Los Nogales winery is still used after that, Montes will need to build themselves another winery to meet projected growth.

# NIGHT PICKING

In 2004, Montes achieved a nocturnal first by harvesting grapes for M and Folly in the very early morning, under generator-powered lamps that were moved around the vineyard. Aurelio borrowed the idea from the Opus One winery in California, who have been night picking for a couple of years, to where he dispatched a trainee to see how it was done. The main reason for night harvesting is that you catch the grapes while they are having their physiological beauty sleep; they lose water in the warmth of the day and rehydrate themselves at night, after which they are more balanced and in generally better shape. A second reason for picking at night is that the grapes' potential to produce alcohol (i.e. level of sugars) is lower if they are picked during the night rather in the daytime, because of the plants' rehydration. Aurelio is a proponent of ripe grapes, but this can lead to alcohol levels approaching 15° by volume that are just too heady. 'By picking grapes at night you can achieve a lower alcohol level with the benefits of full grape ripeness,' says Aurelio.

The new winery at Apalta suffers from a deliberate temperature control problem and one that Aurelio knew would necessitate some night picking. Because Aurelio believes that pumping wine around the winery damages it, he cannot cool grape must by moving it through heat exchangers before maceration. The limitation of the new winery, a good one in Aurelio's view, is that low temperatures cannot be achieved unless they come naturally from the vineyards. Grapes picked during the April or May nights are already at a nicely chilled 11° C, or thereabouts.

*The breaking of dawn signals the end of the first night harvest on the upper slopes of Apalta*

At the lower temperature the fermentation process is slowed, so with less alcohol present, extraction is milder.

The extra cost of picking at night—double the pay plus double the workforce (lamp bearers as well as pickers)—has restricted the practice of night picking to those parcels destined to become M and Folly only. Aurelio is sure the extra cost is worth it, as in his view it results in 'fruitier, delicate and more expressive wines'.

## MONTES' PRODUCTION

| Wine | Denomination of Origin | Approximate annual production - 75 cl bottles |
|------|------------------------|-----------------------------------------------|
| Cabernet Sauvignon Reserve | Colchagua Valley | 960,000 |
| Merlot Reserve | Colchagua Valley | 720,000 |
| Malbec Reserve | Colchagua Valley | 192,000 |
| Chardonnay Reserve | Curicó Valley | 480,000 |

*continued overleaf*

| | | |
|---|---|---|
| Sauvignon Blanc Reserve | Casablanca Valley | 480,000 |
| Cabernet Sauvignon/ Carmenère Limited Selection | Colchagua Valley | 480,000 |
| Pinot Noir Limited Selection | Casablanca Valley | 120,000 |
| Sauvignon Blanc Limited Selection | Leyda Valley | 102,000 |
| Late Harvest, Gewürztraminer/Riesling | Curicó Valley | 4,800 (half bottles) |
| Alpha Cab Sauvignon | Santa Cruz, Colchagua Valley | 1,200,000 |
| Alpha Syrah | Santa Cruz, Colchagua Valley | 360,000 |
| Alpha Merlot | Santa Cruz, Colchagua Valley | 288,000 |
| Alpha Chardonnay | Casablanca Valley | 420,000 |
| Alpha M | Santa Cruz, Colchagua Valley | 19,800 |
| Folly | Santa Cruz, Colchagua Valley | 12,000 |
| Purple Angel | Colchagua Valley | 7,200 |

*Montes Reserve wines were renamed the 'Montes Classic Series' from the 2005 vintage*

# ❧ AURELIO ON HIS FAVOURITE WINES ❧

These are the wines Aurelio considers the best he has produced so far. It is no coincidence that they are also some of the most recent; not because the weather has been significantly better, but because the vineyards are maturing and his knowledge of them growing.

### ALPHA M 2001

'The spring was mild and the summer long and fairly warm, with no early rainfall. So the wines are extremeley concentrated, with wonderfully ripe, polished tannins. This M has layer upon layer of black berry flavours. It is extremely drinkable today. Having said that, 2003 might be even better. We will have to wait a couple of years to see.'

### ALPHA CABERNET 2003

'We had a favourable summer in 2003 with a long dry growing season. Crop thinning was needed. The wine is an intense ruby-red colour. It is lively, with a freshness on the palate and wonderful complexity of flavours. The oak has integrated well.'

### FOLLY 2003

'The Syrah vines at Apalta were ten years old and had achieved their own equilibrium. This wine expresses Syrah character to a huge degree, but with balance – elegant, smooth, but meaty and spicy. Its soft friendly tannins make it sensual. A food wine.'

### ALPHA CHARDONNAY 2004

'Casablanca valley had a rainy winter, followed by a cold spring. The summer weather was fair and we picked before the rain came. It was a long season. Intentionally, the wine underwent less malolactic fermentation. This is an Alpha Chardonnay in a different mould to previous vintages. With higher acidity, it will be able to age longer and develop. It has great potential. The wine is particularly lively and shows lovely individual flavours of pineapple and asparagus.'

### SAUVIGNON (LEYDA) 2005

'Our first vintage from Leyda fruit. It is a knock-out. The clay soils, the sea influence, the constant breezes—they all add up producing a wine with strong varietal flavours and a big mid-palate. This is only the beginning at Leyda. The more we learn the better it will get.'

*A montage of Montes wine awards*

# Chapter 5

# The Angel Spreads her Wings:
## Montes' International Presence

N OT LONG AGO, Montes was an unknown cottage industry operating from the living rooms of its founding partners. It had no permanent address or telephone number and the export department was the contents of Douglas's briefcase. In little over 18 years, Montes has achieved a quite phenomenal feat of growth. Beginning as little more than the hobby of the founding partners, with a modest aim of selling up to 50,000 cases of wine, Montes' success has had an apparent momentum of its own. It is now Chile's fifth largest exporter in terms of value, shipping more than half a million cases to 74 countries. Montes has become a powerful international wine brand, yet it has retained the engaging 'boutique' character of that initial hobby, still driven by the partners' personal passions. According to Pierre Beuchet of Diva, Montes' importer in France (and export agent for stars in France's wine firmament such as JP Moueix, Beaucastel and de Ladoucette), the strength and calibre of Montes' network of worldwide partners is second only to that of Moët & Chandon champagne.

Wine is by nature a convivial product. Its protracted production and maturation allow time for enduring friendships to grow between those who share a passion for and work with it. As former Chairman of Wines of Chile and seemingly just about every export-related wine committee that Chile has had, Douglas's address book of international wine contacts must be the envy of all Chile's wine trade. But he made

*The enigmatic faces of Easter Island's stone inmates, the moai, lure visitors to Montes' remotest domestic outlet. Juan Edmunds Paoa distributes 200 cases annually on Chile's island territory in the Pacific Ocean, located some 3,790 kilometres from the mainland*

a point of not automatically approaching the many importers he had worked with at Viña San Pedro. Commercially, he was aware that the profiles of some of those on the long list of importers with whom he had built up relationships might not fit the winery he and his partners were creating. But, more important for Douglas was his respect for the loyalty of former importers to the Viña San Pedro brand. He felt it was wrong to ask these importers to switch from one wine to another, unless of course they made the first move.

Douglas knew that to break into new markets with such an outlandish thing as Chilean wine, a mentality of selfless dedication was needed. Only recently in 2002 has the promotional body Wines of Chile, collectively funded by Chile's wineries, revitalized itself by opening offices in London and New York. Before that, there was precious little 'brand Chile' promotion to speak of. Success in wine exports has been down to the enterprise of individual concerns, not to a generic campaign to get Chile noticed. 'A lot of people don't even realize that Montes is Chilean,' says Douglas. His worldly view, born of an outward-looking desert upbringing, British roots and a US college education, has helped him adapt and attune himself to the tastes of foreign markets. His commitment has seen him spend a punishing average of seven months out of every 12 away from home for the past decade and a half. By setting his sights further afield, Douglas was able to steal a march on other Chilean wineries at the time, which were mainly used to supplying the relatively undemanding markets of South America. 'When you arrive first, you create double the impact,' says Douglas, of the advantage of being a pioneer in new territories.

The lean export sales team he has recruited now relieves much of the burden: Carlos Serrano, formerly at Viña Undurraga; Eduardo Stark, brand manager; Sonia Montanares, Douglas's ever-loyal former secretary and now in charge of Latin American sales; Vanessa Moreno, his PA for the past 14 years; and Alejandra Ramirez, export assistant. Even so, and mirroring Aurelio's constant re-evaluation of his own winemaking, workaholic Douglas cannot stop. 'Wine has become so competitive at the top end, and it's so important to monitor constantly the feedback from export markets,' he says. Douglas's has been a global crusade, reaching as far as the remote Marquesas Islands of French Polynesia, to spread the Montes word

*Entertaining visitors is part of the job. Douglas and Aurelio lead one of the frequent tractor-pulled tours up the slopes of the Apalta vineyard*

and personally deliver his own unique brand of customer service. It is a level of service that also applies to receiving visitors at home. More often than not, Douglas himself has met the never-ending stream of visitors upon their arrival at Santiago's Merino Benitez airport, and acts as their personal guide to the city, the vineyards, and sometimes beyond, as he did for the artist Ralph Steadman. 'In what other multi-million-dollar business employing nearly 300 people would a founding partner still meet and greet personally?' he asks. 'In the beginning, other wineries in Chile failed to switch to the customer-service-driven philosophy that you need to succeed in wine today,' he says.

As something of a journalist manqué, Douglas has always favoured what now might be considered the rather old-fashioned method of writing personalized letters to potential importers. Letter blitzes on target countries was the simple (but not always effective) way of setting out his stall. 'I once sent off 78 letters to importers in Japan and duly received 78 letters of polite rejection. Only the Japanese would bother to do that,' says Douglas. One missive to India aimed at importer Sanjay Menon did have the intended effect and has since become something of a presentational tool for Montes' persevering agent in the subcontinent. Expressed with Douglas's characteristic modesty the letter began: 'Chile is very far from India, but the distance itself should not deter you from considering our wines, given the success enjoyed by Chilean wines around the world. Please read on...'

*Eye-catching and alluring Alpha advertising in the USA*

The thing was to find new agents of the right size and who shared the same vision. 'The problem is that very few people do the hardest bit: the groundwork research. Even so, once you've got that behind you, all you can do is push with huge effort and hope for the best,' says Douglas. Hoping for the best was the principle at work in June 1989, when a case of Montes' maiden 1987 vintage Cabernet Sauvignon was shipped by air from Santiago to London Heathrow for

*'First, trust. I trusted Aurelio Montes to have the ability to make great wines. Second, wisdom. The wisdom of Douglas Murray to do an outstanding job at marketing the products. He is a passionate and diplomatic individual. Third, our financial guru, Alfred Vidaurre, whose organizing and management of the complicated financial aspects of the winery is amazing.'*

Alex Guarachi, US importer, on why he took on Montes wines

British importer Martin Wright of Hedley Wright. Ten of the 12 bottles broke en route. Martin was able to pick the only two intact samples out of the glass shards and hand-deliver them to the head office of the upmarket wine merchant chain Oddbins. The chain's wine buyer had expressed interest in this new offering from Chile, but was non-committal. He told Martin that he did not know when he would be able to taste the wines, and it was left at that. Not expecting to hear anything for perhaps a couple of weeks, Martin drove for two hours back to his office. There, he was staggered to find a faxed order from Oddbins already sitting on his desk. It was for two sea-containers' worth of the wine that he had just left with the buyer; a resounding 2,000-case vote of confidence in its commercial potential.

This historical snapshot of one transaction amongst the many like it that followed over the years (minus the breakages) illustrates the great swallowing take-up from the wine trades of the first target markets of the UK and the USA. The USA, with its shared sense of American identity in the broadest sense and strong trading links with Chile, was and remains Montes' prime export destination. At the outset, Montes simply did not have the funds to launch in the USA with a national importer as other wineries might have had, so Douglas adopted the slow but sure tactic of gathering importers state by state. He started with California, a wine producing, wine loving state, knowing a favourable response to the wines there would help elsewhere. Other states were soon signed up and before long each importer was asking for the whole country. Cleverly playing them off against each other, Douglas decided that the importer who showed themselves to be the most proactive would win national coverage. In the end, Alex Guarachi of TGIC importers in California took the prize, and reinforced his commitment by buying a small shareholding in Montes.

But Douglas knew that it was success in Britain's more competitive and exigent market conditions that would pave the way for acceptance in other countries. And he got it. British importer Hedley Wright (whose trial, 300-case order was the first ever shipped by Montes) were instrumental in some public

*Aurelio talks viticulture with assembled importers at Marchigüe*

relations bullseyes. These gave Montes a once-only opportunity to grab attention before the market filled up with competing Chilean wineries. In the British national press, revered wine writers such as Oz Clarke extolled the virtues of Aurelio's new Montes Cabernet and Alpha Cabernet under headlines such as 'At last, something concentrated from Chile' and 'The fruity taste of democracy'.

Chile's pariah status under the military regime of General Pinochet had been a great handicap for anything with 'Made in Chile' stamped on it. But after the referendum of 1989 and the return to democracy a year later, Chile came in from the cold. Many markets, particularly those in liberal-minded Europe, opened up to Chilean wine. Douglas now takes quiet satisfaction from the realization of his mini-master plan for Europe: to ship, albeit initially in small quantities, Montes wines to all the continent's wine-producing countries. The greatest triumph is perhaps the presence of Montes Alpha Cabernet and M in the cellars of the 20 Bordeaux restaurants that have the wines on their lists. The last European country to succumb was Greece in 1997, after five years of attritional salesmanship directed at importers Boutari (who now rate Aurelio so highly that they want to collaborate with him on a Greek wine).

When an importer was signed up it was like a feast day. 'You cannot imagine how happy we were,' says Douglas. He, Sonia Montanares and Aurelio would virtually dance round the one telephone they shared in their first, two-roomed office in Santiago's Providencia district. After two years of trading, things had moved a lot quicker than they expected. The number of cases sold in the three years 1989, 1990 and 1991 jumped from 7,000, to 20,000, to 90,000. The sales graph had gone exponential. 'We could have sold more but did not have enough wine,' says Douglas. It would be easy to forget that amidst all this early success Douglas was still selling ceramic tiles. This he was soon able to give up. But taking the long view to a commitment to quality, he and his partners did not take any money out in dividends. Any profits were ploughed straight back into vineyards and the winery.

*Alfredo and his wife Marisa enjoy a break during an early Vinexpo*

The world's great international wine fairs are the ideal meeting point for importers keen to add new wines to their portfolios and for Montes to show the world the fruits of its labours. In an aisle bustling with merchants, hoteliers, sommeliers, restaurateurs, journalists and the occasional freeloader, a handshake, a glass proffered and a couple of mouthfuls of Montes limpid Cabernet created a momentary impression and lasting business relationship for several Montes importers. Dutch agent Marnix Engels recalls Aurelio and Douglas standing shyly behind their exhibitor's table at their first Vinexpo in 1991, where he was instantly impressed by an exposure of fruit in the Sauvignon Blanc and Cabernet Sauvignon (awarded gold and silver medals, respectively) that 'you did not find in the traditional world'. Back home, the partners' wives, Lucy (Douglas's), Bernardita (Aurelio's), Marisa (Alfredo's) and Josette (Pedro's), were in the meantime selling small quantities of Montes to Santiago's upmarket restaurants. Armed with the wine sales experience, at later fairs they would often help man the stands. The feminine touch certainly worked on Brazilian importer Ciro Lilla, who admits that he was as impressed by the wives as he was by the wines.

On top of the wines, the combination of Douglas's and Aurelio's charm and the personal attention they have given to the Montes project have endeared them to many and have undoubtedly contributed to their success. 'They are people's people and everyone loves them,' say Marnix Engels. Importers across the world talk of the 'family' feeling and the spirit of collaborative association that Montes engenders, symbolized by the Angel. (In Japan, Douglas is addressed as 'Papa' by his importers Enoteca and he considers Chinese importer Johnny Chan to be a blood brother.) As Dmitry Pinski, Montes' Russian importer, puts it: 'The Montes winery has a different kind of approach, it's very personalized and very positive. The whole team is motivated towards success. And these things are contagious.'

But Douglas's unbridled enthusiasm for his product occasionally landed him in trouble. Believing that every little bit of marketing helps, he has a habit of introducing himself to anyone, anywhere, he sees drinking Montes. Shortly after beginning to export to Russia, he was having dinner with Dmitry Pinski at Moscow's well-heeled Pushkin restaurant, a favourite of local politicos. Having spotted a bottle of Alpha Cabernet on a neighbouring table, unannounced, Douglas got up from his seat and made for its distinguished-looking female imbiber. Out of nowhere, two burly figures suddenly appeared. They lifted Douglas up by his armpits, and thrust him up against the wall, his feet dangling helplessly. History does not relate whom the minders were protecting, but Dmitry quickly intervened and apprised Douglas of the inherent risk in approaching strangers at expensive restaurants in Russia's new economy.

Douglas used every possible trick to help spread Montes. The cloak of immunity conferred on the diplomatic bags of Chile's foreign embassies was one useful way of getting samples of wine past tricky customs officials in some countries. Now it's official: Montes wines are available to Chilean ambassadors on new postings thanks to an official arrangement with the Chilean Ministry of Foreign Affairs.

**LUNCHEON**

In Honour of
His Excellency Mr. Ricardo LAGOS Escobar,
President of the Republic of Chile

Hosted by
The Japan Chamber of Commerce and Industry
Japanese National Committee
of the Japan-Chile Business Co-operation Committee
Supported by
Nippon Keidanren
Keizai Doyukai
Japan Foreign Trade Council, Inc.

February 14, 2003

Hotel New Otani

Champagne — Pommery Brut Royal
White Wine — Montes Alpha Chardonnay 2001, Chile
Red Wine — Montes Alpha Cabernet Sauvignon 1997, Chile

*Alphas Chardonnay and Cabernet Sauvignon doing their bit for Chilean-Japanese relations—menu of a lunch given in honour of visiting Chilean President Ricardo Lagos by the Japanese Chamber of Commerce and Industry in 2003*

*Of the numerous accolades Alpha Chardonnay has received, none was of better publicity for Douglas than the 1998 vintage being voted 'Best Chardonnay in the World'. In February 2000, the Slow Food Movement and Vinitaly wine fair organized a simultaneous global tasting of Chardonnay (allowing for time differences), called 'The Game of Pleasure'. In 25 countries, 1,300 wine writers, sommeliers and enthusiasts polled their votes on six Chardonnays tasted blind. The Alpha emerged the clear winner, ahead of Chardonnays from Coldstream Hills of Australia, Mondavi of California, Golan Heights Winery of Israel, Tenimenti Ruffino of Italy, and Sieur D'Arques of southern France. However, the Italian entrants were unhappy with the result and lodged a complaint. So at Vinitaly 2000 a month later, a second 'test' was carried out by the Italian Sommelier Association, the result of which was the ratification of the Alpha Chardonnay's clear victory*

On the wider diplomatic front, a series of beneficial free-trade agreements have been forged between Chile and its important trading partners. Previously punitive tariffs slapped on Chilean goods entering the USA and Canada, Korea and, most recently, the European Union are progressively being reduced to nil. For a country that in the 1980s exported only five per cent of its wine production and now, remarkably, exports nearer 60 per cent, these pacts bring a welcome degree of security. They should bring to an end previous quota squabbles and politically motivated blockades and hindrances, such as the notorious case in 1989 of three cyanide-laced table grapes allegedly found in the USA by health officials, which cost the Chilean fruit industry $300 million in lost revenue and led to a dispute that continued for a decade.

At the sharp end of diplomacy, Montes wines may well have helped oil the wheels of international discourse. At home, Montes' all-Chilean pedigree may be a factor in its favoured place in the cellars of La Moneda, Santiago's Presidential Palace. In Brazil, before uproar from the country's nascent wine industry halted the habit, Montes Alpha was the preferred choice of President Cardoso. (After serving it to visiting President Chirac of France, local producers said enough was enough.) In Hong Kong, before the handover of the British colony to China, consignments of Alpha Cabernet Sauvignon and Alpha Chardonnay were regularly delivered to

Government House, on the instructions of the last British Governor and Montes fan, Christopher Patten. In China itself, Montes Alpha was the wine served at the state banquet given in honour of Chile's ex-President Frei when he visited the country, during which he autographed a bottle of Alpha Cabernet, adding his own imprimatur next to Aurelio's preprinted signature on the label. And Aurelio knew he and Montes had arrived in Hong Kong when the receptionist at the Mandarin Hotel asked him if he really was *the* Aurelio Montes and asked him for his autograph.

Perhaps the greatest sea change in wine-drinking habits on which Montes has capitalized is the one that taken place in the markets of East Asia: Japan, Korea, China, Hong Kong, Thailand, Malaysia, Vietnam and Singapore. Barely ten years ago, wine was a cultural import for these territories' elites; whisky, rice beer and sake were what most people drank. In the region's top hotels (which some consider the world's best), French wines were available and their distribution was in the hands of powerful French drinks groups such as the giant Rémy Martin. Shipping a container of wine from the Chilean port of Valparaíso to Hong Kong cost about five times as much as one from France; and on top of that, import taxes were stingingly high. The chances of getting a toe-hold in hotels and restaurants with a Chilean wine were virtually non-existent. As a great believer in developing parallel markets alongside the mainstream, Douglas had been there, tub-thumping, 20 years before that and felt at home. 'I visited the Far East so much partly because I fell in love with it,' he says. 'It just looked so different—the plants, the people, even the colour of the sky.' The creeping westernization and changing consumer tastes in these growing economies provided fertile ground for wine-drinking to flourish. In particular, salaried women, emancipated from their traditional, subordinate roles, began to spend their disposable incomes on wine—especially white wine—attracted by its sophisticated, aspirational image. In the 1990s, as supply met demand, ocean freight costs plummeted and the region opened up as virgin sales territory. Although Douglas had an instinct for the Far East's potential as a new consumer bloc, even he did not foresee the boom that would follow: Japan, China and Korea now equal or

*Chinese importer Johnny Chan clutches his angel-bearing wines in Lhasa, Tibet*

surpass North America or Europe as recipients of Chilean exports. But he maintains that 'rather than seeing Asia as simply another marketplace to do business in, I have tried to understand their cultures'. In the so-called 'immature' wine markets of east Asia, Montes and Montes Alpha wine have had the advantage of pronounceable and memorable names, of an appealing generosity of flavours and fruit based on a French model; overall, of sticking power with new wine drinkers.

Fortune has smiled on Montes and Chile, with events having given unexpected boosts to sales figures. In the mid-1990s, the US importer of the Chilean giant Concha y Toro, Excelsior, was bought by the even larger Italian producer Villa Banfi, quickly increasing awareness of Chilean wines across the States. In 1995, France's widely condemned unilateral decision to conduct nuclear tests on the Pacific atoll of Muroroa resulted in a complete boycott of French goods in Japan. France's virtual stranglehold there on the supply of quality wine was loosened. Douglas presided over the first trade delegation that followed. In a repetition of its historical role of filling the supply gap when the flow of wine in France has been interrupted (as happened during the phylloxera crisis in the nineteenth century and in the 1950s during the Algerian war) Chile filled the void with Cabernet Sauvignon that has remained popular with the Japanese ever since. The only difference now in Japan and elsewhere is that Chilean wines such as Montes are no longer considered Bordeaux substitutes. They stand on their own. Indeed in Asia and elsewhere Douglas believes the problems are not over for French wines. 'The prices of classed-growth clarets are a problem for sommeliers,' he says. The wine waitering profession is a well-organized, international one, whose members working in the hotels and restaurants of the Far East have mostly learnt their wines in the USA, so they are well aware of what Chile offers. 'Sommeliers network and share information,' says Douglas. 'And now they almost prefer not to sell French wines, because their prices have recently been so erratic. The cost of replacing a top French wine can be too high and we have benefited from that situation. I believe this is a big problem for the French.' Montes' strategy has been to keep the prices in local currencies stable, and it has worked.

Japan's interest in the wines of its distant Pacific neighbour has attracted film crews to Chile on several occasions. On one visit, some of the leading wineries failed to grasp the PR potential of the moment and were either haughty or luke-warm in their reception of their visitors, especially as it was a Sunday. Montes alone achieved a public relations coup after Douglas, in typical style, greeted his guests personally and showed the respect that goes down well with the etiquette-conscious Japanese. The result was invaluable prime-time exposure for Montes on Japanese television, fronted by one of the country's most popular celebrity actresses, Misa Shimizu. Indeed,

Douglas's relationship with Japan is such that it has gone beyond the Montes brand. His influence on the vinous habits of this relatively novice wine-drinking country are such that in 2000 Japan's oldest wine trade magazine, *Vinothèque,* selected him as one of the six wine world personalities who have most influenced the Japanese wine market.

In Korea, Montes got a huge kick-start during the Football World Cup of 2002. The importer Nara Foods, keen to make progress after the 1999 Asian financial crisis, sent samples of Alpha Cabernet to the organizing committee, who were planning the menu and

*Douglas and Eduardo Stark take a small tea break in a traditional Korean tea house with importers Nara Foods*

wine list for the event's inaugural dinner in the city of Busan. The Alpha was chosen, after which a Korean television film crew descended on Montes' vineyards, from where reports were broadcast on Korean national television over several days. Since then, the Korean thirst for Montes appears unquenchable. According to Hi-Sang Lee of Nara Foods, Montes wines are 'ordered as frequently as water' in 'almost every restaurant'. No wonder Korea is now Douglas's number two importer in the region after Japan, and fifth in the world.

The apparent health benefits of red wine have helped in the Asian markets and elsewhere. Red wine's life-enhancing qualities have been pinned down to antioxidants and flavonoids, the flavour-producing compounds that can reduce the risk of blood clots and heart disease. After undergoing heart surgery in the early 1990s, Thailand's popular King Bhumibol Adulyadej declared that his doctor allowed him to drink only red wine, as it would aid his recovery. The king's loyal subjects followed his example and Thai wine-drinking habits changed

'*For Dan Murphy it has primarily been the people involved in Montes who set Montes apart from its contemporaries. It keeps coming back to their passion and pride in their product. This naturally comes through in the bottle and is the soul of their wines…Montes are more to us than business associates, they are cherished friends.*'

Greta Coghill, of Australian importer Dan Murphy, on Montes

dramatically overnight, as the country switched from drinking predominantly white wine to red. Meanwhile in Britain, in 2003, government National Health Service doctors at Great Western Hospital in Swindon started to administer Chilean Cabernet to patients on the cardiac ward. Thanks to Chile's strong Andean light and wide night-day temperature swings, her Cabernet

*Brand building in China*

contains significantly greater quantities of the health-promoting chemicals than reds from other regions. The doctors' prescription was Montes Reserve Cabernet Sauvignon (properly dispensed in wine glasses!) and it made headlines in the national papers.

Wine's benign character is one apparent reason for it catching on in the market with the biggest potential of them all: China. Montes' importer in the stirring giant is Johnny Chan, former Chairman of the Hong Kong Wine Club and author of the first book on table wines written in Mandarin. He has been instrumental not only in establishing Montes in the high-end outlets of Shanghai and Beijing (and the high-altitude outlets of Tibet), but also in developing an interesting Sino-Chilean vinous axis between the government's wine and spirit directorate COFCO (the China National Cereals, Oils & Foodstuffs Import & Export Corporation) and Montes. Keen to promote wine as a healthier alternative to spirits made from grain (which would be better used to feed China's myriad hungry mouths) COFCO have held up Montes' approachable wines as benchmarks against which the products from China's own vineyards be judged. Bare-shouldered pin-up photographs of bottles of Alpha M and Folly were even featured on the COFCO 2003 calendar.

'The challenging part of marketing Chilean wines has been trying to convince, not so much the trade—who trust you—but the press and the experts, that Chile can produce great wines,' Douglas contends. Press files in Douglas's office bulge with laudatory cuttings assiduously gathered by importers and local PR agencies employed across four continents. They attest to an overwhelmingly welcoming approval, often rapturous, of what Montes (and Chile) has achieved. But this is frequently expressed in terms of a virtue from which Douglas and his

*In 2002, Chile's 'Group of Five' top producers went on a US roadshow to collectively explain and promote their new high-end wines. From left, at New York's Daniel Restaurant (where M was launched four years earlier): Agustín Huneeus of Veramonte, Rafael Guilisasti of Concha y Toro, Aurelio Montes, Eduardo Chadwick of Errazuriz, Tim Mondavi, then of Seña, and Steven Spurrier, the British wine writer, who presided*

partners would, fundamentally, prefer to disassociate themselves: value for money. The creation of M and Folly were expressions of Montes' ultimate ambition to produce wines that deserved to be expensive.

Confidence in Project X, the secretive proto-title of the wine that became M, grew after barrel samples of the first 1996 vintage were discreetly exhibited at Vinexpo in 1997, much to the surprise and delight of several visitors. Its public unveiling as M in February 1998, priced in the USA at more than $55 a bottle, was the cause of trepidation behind the scenes. They had built a strong platform with the Alpha range. But even so, M was a very high-risk venture. This was not just in monetary terms, but because of the damage any failure could have done to Montes' overall image as a producer. A staggered launch in key cities was planned. It was so important that things went smoothly in New York, London, Tokyo and San Francisco that the first launch, a kind of practice run, was held in São Paulo, Brazil, after which a useful feedback debrief was held with assembled sommeliers. Time was somewhat of the essence, as close on the heels of Montes was the Mondavi-Chadwick joint venture with their own signature ultra-premium wine, Seña. Montes were keen to be the first to launch, proudly affirming that theirs was a 100-per-cent Chilean wine, not the product of an international collaboration. New York, close to where the majority of American wine writers live, was chosen as the city to launch properly what was to be Chile's most expensive wine in its 450-year-old winemaking history. 'Unlike the Seña launch, we avoided a social, black-tie affair,' says Douglas. 'We wanted to place the emphasis firmly on the wine and show the wine to people who mattered. The formation of the tasting room tables was like a classroom, and Aurelio and Douglas presented the wine like a play before critics. A vertical flight of Alpha Cabernets going back to the original 1987 was tasted, whose impressive bottle-ageing was in itself engaging to the critics, leading up to the M itself. Aurelio and Douglas spoke and tried to explain what the M meant to Chile and to Montes ('A wine comparable to California's Opus One at half the price,' says Douglas).

In the States, the critics were united in their admiration for the quality of M. *Wine Enthusiast* described it as 'extraordinarily rich, concentrated and Margaux-like...with a finish that goes on and on' but imputed the high price as a means of being taken seriously. The *Wine Spectator* praised the wine for standing 'apart from other super-Chileans for its understated elegance' but later baulked rather at the price tag, declaring 'Sticker Shock from Chile'. After its launch in Britain, *Decanter* magazine bracketed Montes in the 'Cloud Cuckoo Gang' (along with Mondavi-Chadwick and others) who 'took it upon themselves to rip up the price rule book'.

*Douglas in heaven with Purple Angels at the Mexican launch of the wine in Mérida*

Douglas believes that most wine magazines and writers at that time did not believe Chile could produce quality, and that they tried to find disqualifiers (an easy one being the price) rather than virtues. The American wine press's points system for marking wine out of 100 seemed to him to reflect this. This wine scoring, although decried by those who say it is meaningless to judge wine by numbers, is a commercial fact of life. It cannot be ignored by producers such as Montes whose main market is the USA. To the outsider, small differences in points awarded take on what seems a disproportionate significance. But to producers they can mean everything. The first vintage of M was awarded 89 points by the *Wine Spectator*. When Folly came out it received 92 points. Douglas contends that 'by then the editors had made up their minds that Chile really could produce wines of a higher level'. Be that as it may, the important question was, had Douglas and Aurelio read the market correctly? Had they produced a wine for which the consumer was prepared to pay the sum asked? The facts speak for themselves: importers worldwide had no trouble selling M. The prestige-label-driven market of Hong Kong was a good case in point. According to importer Rob Temple, 'the arrival

*The Hong Kong-based Chinese newspaper* Ta Kung Pao, *decoratively introduces Douglas and explains Alpha M and Folly to its readers in June 2002*

of Alpha was the first time that wine drinkers looked up from their Bordeaux and said "this is serious stuff..." Montes recreated this revolution with the advent of M. Again, it was considered by many to be almost foolhardy to attempt to sell a Chilean wine above HK$500 in Hong Kong regardless of quality, and yet the first cases of M to arrive here were snapped up in a matter of days. Consumers were astounded by the quality'. As the vines of Apalta have aged and Aurelio's knowledge of the vineyard has deepened, the quality and the reputation of the wine has improved with each vintage. The world's supplies of M are now strictly rationed on a country-by-country basis.

Montes chose to put itself through stage fright again, four years after the launch of M, when the 2000 Folly made its debut. The player they had introduced to the performance this time, and the cause for trepidation, was a new variety in Chile: Syrah.

*'When I received the first pallet of Montes wines (Douglas's idea) there were ten cases of Montes Alpha M. I said to myself: "He is mad. How can I sell a Chilean wine that nobody knows, at this crazy price?" I did some rough calculations and decided to sell the other wines and make enough money to buy for myself those ten cases of M. But I sold them in a week. My cellar is still lacking.'*

María Emilia Campos, Portuguese importer

The wine-drinking world had become accustomed to the expensive ultra-premium Chileans such as M. But an ultra-premium Syrah was a radical departure from Chile's inheritance of Bordeaux-style wines; the grape had been in Chile barely ten years and, apart from on the slopes of Apalta, it had an unproven track record. Knowing that the concept of 'icon' wines goes down better in the USA than perhaps elsewhere, New York was again chosen as the launch city and 65 invitations were sent out. Those on the guest list included three editors from the *Wine Spectator*, two Chilean ambassadors and, amongst others, James Halliday, the influential Australian writer and winemaker.

*The Folly Angel makes her debut*

The day before the launch, Marsha Palanci of Cornerstone Communications, Montes' PR in the USA, called Douglas to say 'that the most incredible thing is happening. People are asking for invitations to come'. In the end, it was a sell-out. Unusually, everyone who was invited came, plus a couple of extras. The artist Ralph Steadman, painter of Folly's Atacama desertscapes, was there and remembers 'the sky was grey, and the mood was very optimistic but apprehensive. Douglas and Aurelio were very nervous. It was like the first night of a new ballet'. After tasting a wine that was unimaginably pure, intense and well-balanced, no-one said anything. Then someone started to clap and applause quickly broke out around the room. 'Aurelio had invented a new way for Syrah,' says Steadman. Douglas felt he had touched wine heaven and a shiver went down his spine. Aurelio lit a large cigar. Needless to say, James Halliday was as impressed as anyone that day and on his return home wrote a piece in *The Weekend Australian* saying 'Obviously enough, it is a very youthful wine, years away from its peak. But it is technically perfect and... proclaims its quality.'

*Douglas, Marsha Palanci, Montes' PR in the USA, and label artist Ralph Steadman, let their hair down after the Folly launch at New York's Daniel restaurant in 2002*

Montes' precocious commercial success has not gone unnoticed by business academia. As part of a broader study of the Chilean wine industry, MBA students at the well-respected Kellogg School of Management of Northwestern University in Illinois decided to analyse Montes' strategy. Under scrutiny were the different marketing tactics adopted by four of Chile's leading producers. Douglas and his colleagues were flattered by the attention, but there was not much to learn from results of the study. The unremarkable conclusion was a rubber-stamping: as a premium wine producer, Montes and its importers were doing everything right in placing its wines in upmarket wine stores and restaurants.

Such is their business success that Aurelio and Douglas were selected to be mentors of the 2004 Wine MBA course, a recently established programme run jointly by four institutions: Bordeaux Business School, the University of California at Davis, Santiago's Catholic University and the University of South Australia at Adelaide. The course is designed to equip today's wine marketeers with a perspective and understanding that befits what has become a pan-global industry. The course's previous two mentors were Robert Mondavi and Baroness Philippine de Rothschild—Aurelio's and Douglas's joint-selection as the third speaks volumes about the place Montes has earned at the heart of the wine establishment. In his mentor's speech at Bordeaux to the graduating class of 2004, Douglas concluded with the following simple advice: 'Remember this: no-one ever achieved fame by imitation. People and producers who have greatly influenced the wine world are those who have dared to do things differently.'

*The influential US wine magazine* Wine Enthusiast *named Montes New World Winery of the Year in 2002. (Other contending producers included Penfolds of Australia, Villa Maria of New Zealand and KWV of South Africa.) Michael Schachner,* Wine Enthusiast *Contributing Editor, explains why: 'Montes stands out for two main reasons. One is the fact that it began as a privately financed upstart not even 20 years ago, and today it sells its wines literally worldwide. The owners are quintessential frequent fliers, and no potential export market will be ignored. Two is the wines themselves. Across a broad spectrum, Montes wines are usually at the top of their class. And with respect to the highest-end cuvées, these compete with the best the world has to offer'*

*Douglas reveals the Order of the Angel, first awarded to loyal friends of Montes at a Marchigüe lunch, on the occasion of the opening of the Apalta winery*

It is a matter of huge satisfaction and pride for the Montes partners to see how far they have reached in such a short time. 'It has been an uphill task trying to persuade wine critics that Chile has the potential to produce really world-class wines such as M and Folly. But I think we have done that,' Douglas says. 'We now have to wait for what I believe is the last hurdle. That is to demonstrate that the top wines now being made have the capacity to age. Perhaps 15 to 20 years from now, Chilean wines will have proved that they can last the distance.' Then, and only then, will the partners' vision truly be realized: when the world sees Chile as they do—as a world-class wine producer. The Angel is watching.

# ∼ THE WINGSPAN ∼

## MONTES' WORLDWIDE DISTRIBUTION, WITH YEAR OF FIRST SHIPMENT

| 1989 | 1992 (continued) |
|---|---|
| USA | Sweden |
| UK | Colombia |
| **1990** | **1993** |
| Japan | Mexico |
| Canada | New Caledonia |
| **1991** | Paraguay |
| Brazil | Barbados |
| Germany | Finland |
| Puerto Rico | Thailand |
| Netherlands | Ecuador |
| Ireland | Peru |
| South Africa | Iceland |
| France | **1994** |
| Uruguay | India |
| New Zealand | Kenya |
| **1992** | Luxembourg |
| Spain | Hong Kong |
| Italy | New Guinea |
| Denmark | **1995** |
| Belgium | Korea |
| Venezuela | Philippines |
| Switzerland | French Polynesia |
| Australia | Turkey |
| Norway | Macau |

## 1995 (continued)

China

Singapore

## 1996

Falkland Islands

Austria

Holy See Vatican City

Argentina

## 1997

Taiwan

Trinidad & Tobago

Greece

United Arab Emirates

The Bahamas

Dominican Republic

## 1998

Malaysia

Lebanon

## 1999

Indonesia

## 2000

Russia

## 2001

Bermuda

Estonia

Cyprus

Panama

Israel

Portugal

## 2002

Vietnam

Malta

## 2004

Costa Rica

Czech Republic

Cayman Islands

British Virgin Islands

Jamaica

Guatemala

Poland

Ukraine

Cook Islands

## ∾ IMPORTER TESTIMONIALS ∾

'*Over the past 10 or so years, Chilean wines have gained significant market share in Mexico. Our own Mexican wine sells most and for several years Spain occupied the number two slot. But that place has now been taken by Chile, mostly with wines of standard quality at low cost. Montes Alpha was the pioneer in our market in offering outstanding quality at affordable prices. Montes stands out because the personal attention given by the partners to all their clients, and to clients of their clients, is outstanding. We have been honored to distribute Montes, Montes Alpha, M and Folly.*'

**Jorge García**
Casa Cuervo, Mexico

'*In the early 1990s I was looking for a Chilean wine to add to our portfolio—a high quality wine with the right people behind it. We were instantly impressed by Montes Alpha Cabernet Sauvignon, by its fruit, its depth and its ripeness.*

*All members of our staff are touched by the 'Montes spirit', which for us means passion, enthusiasm and honour. We value highly the Montes team's professionalism and friendship.*'

**Y.Hirose**
Enoteca, Japan

'*Viña Montes stands out because of their innovation, their preoccupation with quality, their close personal approach and their first-class vineyards at Apalta. Montes Alpha Cabernet Sauvignon is classed in Brazil as if it were a Bordeaux wine and can be found on all good dining tables in the country.*'

**Ciro Lilla**
Mistral, Brazil

'*Our wine portfolio includes mostly family or privately-owned companies. With the consolidation going on in the wine trade, and the highly leveraged financial position of the large companies, too much emphasis is often put on volume at any price. Montes is a long-term quality-oriented producer, and very focused on delivering consistent quality. That is consistent with our own business philosophy.*

*Montes remains a relatively small seller in Canada compared to the major shippers, such as Concha y Toro. However, among quality shippers Montes ranks among the most prominent, thanks to the excellent press coverage both in Canada and internationally, as well as the personal visits of the Montes export team.'*

Michel Marentette
Whitehall, Canada

'*We came in contact with Montes way back in 1991, when there was no wine culture to speak of in India. Imports were restricted to those 5-star hotels with licences issued to them exclusively against their foreign exchange earnings. The volumes were very small indeed and almost all of it French.*

*Montes wines were the first Chilean wines on the Indian market. Many other wines are now available, but for a long time Montes was the wine served exclusively at official Chilean functions. The Indian wine market is still small and difficult. But Douglas has always encouraged us with his fabulous missives, that are always honest and from the heart.'*

Sanjay Menon
Sonarys, India

'*I first met Douglas Murray at Vinexpo in 1989. Our company at that time was too small to import a complete container of wines from Chile. Douglas, however, visited us whenever he was in the area, wrote letter after letter and, finally, we decided to contact a couple of partners and we managed to put a first mixed container together of 12,000 bottles.*

*In 1992, we and other importers founded the 'Vereinigung zur Förderung chilenischer Weine in der Schweiz', an association for promoting Chilean wines in Switzerland. In 1994, we were able to take a booth with five other exhibitors at the annual Expovina in Zurich. Today, almost every Swiss restaurant has wines from Chile on its list and Montes is one of the best-known producers.'*

Jürg Reinger
Haecky, Switzerland

'*Montes wines were introduced eleven years ago after an encounter with Pedro Grand, who was on vacation Tahiti. Besides the quality of the Montes wines, I was impressed by the dedication that Douglas showed for a relatively modest market such as Tahiti. Being a French-based culture, our general preference is for the wines of France. It is quite a task changing that habit with wines of different origins. No-one would take the risk of importing a premium wine from Chile. After tasting Montes, we decided to accept the challenge and are very satisfied with the result, as some other distributors are now following in our steps.'*

**Clet Wong**
Sodispo, French Polynesia

*'When I met all four partners in Chile in 1989, I was struck by their enthusiasm, their willingness to learn about the requirements of the UK market, their determination to succeed, and their true desire to pursue excellence in winemaking. They were neither timid nor bold—they had a strong vision and were committed to it. They seemed to want to challenge the norm, push back some boundaries, and see how good Chilean wine could get. They were always interested, friendly, amazingly hospitable, and were the very best people that I ever worked with in the wine trade.'*

**Martin Wright**
HwCg, UK

# Index

# PHOTOGRAPH CREDITS

Ángel Cabeza Monteira, Chilean National Monuments Council  4
Aurelio Montes  15
Sara Matthews  vi, 16, 34b, 40, 49, 50t, 72, 96
Elysia Moon  94
Douglas Murray  21, 92, 95
Jamie Ross  viii, 19, 20, 30, 34t, 37, 41, 47, 50b, 51
ShutterStock  2, 12, 84
Ralph Steadman  65
*Ta Kung Pao*  98
Alfredo Vidaurre  ii, 22, 24, 45b, 46, 89
Wines of Chile  8, 9, 19t, 38, 45t
*Wine Enthusiast*  100

Montes SA, all other images

Photograph captions for preliminary pages:
page ii – Montes' El Arcángel de Marchigüe estate
page vi – Inside the Los Nogales bodega
page viii – Montes' La Finca de Apalta estate

English version ISBN 956-8077-73-1
Spanish version ISBN 956-8077-72-3

Printed in China on behalf of Origo Ediciones

Text © Jamie Ross 2006
Copyright © Montes 2006
Designed by Richard Pierce

Published by:
Montes SA
Av. Del Valle 945, Of 2611
Ciudad Empresarial
Huechuraba
Santiago, Chile
www.monteswines.com